A Walk on the Breakwater

with 'God's Mate' and an 'Ordinary Chaplain'

by
GEORGE O'BRIEN

Copyright © 2019 George O'Brien

First published in 2019
Reprinted in 2020 and 2022

The right of George O'Brien to be identified as the Author of this Work has been asserted by him in accordance with the Copyright, Designs and Patents Act 1988.

All rights reserved. No part of this publication may be reproduced, stored in a retrieval system or transmitted, in any form or by any means, without the prior written permission of the publisher.

Unless otherwise marked, Scripture quotations are taken from The Authorised (King James) Version. Rights in the Authorised Version in the United Kingdom are vested in the Crown. Reproduced by permission of the Crown's patentee, Cambridge University Press (www.cambridge.org).

Scripture quotations marked 'NIV' are taken from The Holy Bible, New International Version (Anglicised edition). Copyright © 1976, 1984, 2011 by Biblica (formerly International Bible Society). Used by permission of Hodder & Stoughton Publishers, an Hachette UK company. All rights reserved.

The hymns 'In Loving-kindness Jesus Came' and 'When All My Labours and Trials Are O'er' (by Charles Hutchinson Gabriel 1856–1932), 'Come, Thou Fount of Every Blessing' (by Robert Robinson 1735–1790), 'Have You Any Room for Jesus?' (adapted by Daniel W. Whittle 1840–1901), 'O For a Closer Walk with God' (by William Cowper 1731–1800) and 'How Good is the God We Adore' (by J. Hart 1712–1768) from which quotes are taken are in the Public Domain.

ISBN: 978-1-910719-76-3

Design and Print management by Verité CM Ltd

www.veritecm.com

Cover picture © Seven Wave Gallery, Bude. 01288 356935

Printed in England

DEDICATION

In memory of William and Florence Davey

of 'Hamvale', Hillhead, Stratton, North Cornwall

evacuation foster parents 1940–1942

WHAT OTHERS SAY

Awash with affectionate memories. So rich a picture of the past, and of the formative influences of special people not least the remarkable Davey's. **Adrian Whitfield QC**

There are parallels to my own story, but I wouldn't have the boldness and honesty to put them on paper. **Rev. Tom Sharp**

Just to say how much I have enjoyed and appreciated 'A Walk on the Breakwater', so honest, humorous and very moving. **Elizabeth Clarke**

I am able still to get excited by spiritual memories. Your book made me feel young again. **Myra Leslie**

Your excellent book is very readable, a strong sense of God's love and guidance. **David Farrer**

I'm happily reading your memoirs. **William Parker**

The cover and title of the book put me in a pleasant mood before I started to read. A breakwater is a defined point between two environments land and sea or metaphorically the past and future, good and bad, faith and doubt, belief and disbelief and there are many more examples. The picture is similarly ambivalent is Sun setting or rising? The two threads that ran through the book are faith and philosophical questioning. **Andy McNaughton**

PREFACE

As a young schoolboy I remember sitting by a front-room window producing a piece of homework for Miss Jackson my English teacher, knowing instinctively that it was an acceptable piece of prose. What it was about I can't recall, I just knew it felt right! I have seemed able to hold my own in the literacy stakes – a report written when Secretary of the Fulham 'Calling Youth Campaign' in 1960 was well received; our annual Christmas letters also seem to be appreciated.

I hope these memoirs will have a similar effect. Preparing and planning them has been spread over many years. Collecting, collating material and photographs has been pleasurable, especially so as in my forties (1972–1982), during times of black depression, I destroyed many papers and manuscripts relating to my childhood and teenage years.

Fortunately my wife Mary compensated and kept much correspondence from 1959–1962, which has been invaluable and revealing. Relatives and friends have helped piece together other aspects of my past. 'Ancestry', the online family website, has been invaluable. I discovered a favourite uncle had been twice married and my own father had been conceived out of wedlock, his mother dying when he was only fifteen.

Chapters will develop personal and psychological aspects of my life. We shall visit many places: Dagenham, London; Bude and Stratton, North Cornwall; Brentwood, Essex; Harringay Arena; Huntingdon; Finsbury Square; Bristol; Carlisle; Stafford.

Hopefully these memoirs can be completed, printed and distributed in 2019. This will be a cause of celebration and thanks to Almighty God for His hand upon one who has walked with Him on the breakwater of life.

A number of 'typos' (wrong dates and misspellings, e.g. bowel for bowl p.42!) were found in the first printing October 2019.

In correcting them I have taken the opportunity of adding some extra material in two particular areas viz Theological education and Poetry as an aid to personal spiritual growth.

These additional essays will be found in the addendumn – although referred to elsewhere in the book (pages 66 and 137). I hope these extra items with a Prayer of commitment (Page 144) and 'What others say' will add to the usefulness of the book

George O'Brien September 2020

CONTENTS

Introduction 9

1. My First Step on the Breakwater 11

2. Evacuation 1940–1943 25

3. Return to London 37

4. Billy Graham Crusade, Harringay Arena.
   Bristol, Training for Ministry 49

5. 1964–1968: Carlisle – Stafford 69

6. Moving from Carlisle (1964–1968) to Stafford (1968–1988) 79

7. Chaplaincy 1988–1999 95

8. 1999 Onwards: Retirement Years 103

9. What Makes Me Tick? Psychology and All That 119

10. Allotment, Probus, Poetry, Books, Sermons and Heaven 133

Addendum 143

INTRODUCTION

A 'walk on the breakwater' is a way of describing my life; when it started and what happened throughout eighty-seven years. 'God's Mate' and an 'Ordinary Chaplain'[1] speak of a relationship and purpose. For me, that means knowing God and being a Christian minister.

The breakwater in question breaks up the Atlantic rollers in Bude, North Cornwall. It was first built between 1839 and 1843, the current one's a second construction, the first having been washed away a few years after it was built. I first walked on it as an evacuee in 1940.

During the Second World War (1939–1945) my brother Charlie and I were evacuated from London. For many children, being evacuated during the war was a difficult experience. For us it was a meaningful time. We had nothing but praise for the good people who cared for us.

Life can be viewed as a walk or journey, having a direction and a destination. This life is not all; there is a future and a hope which motivates us. Jesus Christ spoke of people being either on a narrow or broad way: one way leads to life, the other to destruction. The path has been prepared; it is for us to walk along it.

A walk on a breakwater can be a delightful experience, salty smelling sea spray in your nostrils, lapping waves rushing over interlocking stones then pouring back and starting again. But a walk starts somewhere. The Chinese proverb says, 'A thousand mile journey begins with one step.' So do you fancy 'a walk on the breakwater' with me?

....

[1] Anecdotally speaking. The terms 'Gods Mate' and 'Ordinary Chaplain' refer to actual incidents covered in this book.

CHAPTER 1

My First Step on the Breakwater

'A thousand mile journey begins with one step.'

. . . .

Metaphorically speaking I took my first step towards the Breakwater in 1932, my birth year. It was a momentous year.

There was anti-British violence in India. Gandhi was arrested and threatened a hunger strike to death. Sixty-six thousand Indians were arrested and convicted of civil disobedience.

British soldiers were in action in Iraq to quell a rebellion of Kurds in the North.

In Germany presidential elections were held and Adolf Hitler was a candidate; the Nazi Party continued to do well and demanded Germany's release from the shackles of the Versailles Treaty. Hitler eventually became Chancellor in January 1933.

In the USA there was the Great Depression and unemployment reached eleven million.

The League of Nations sought to control the aggressive acts of various nations, including Japan's advance into Manchuria.

In China Mao Tse-tung and the Communist Party were growing in strength and influence, and in the Soviet Union Stalin's reign of terror and oppression had begun.

Into this world I was born. My older brother Kenneth Charles (Charlie) had been born on 21st January 1931 at 5, Redan

On my Father's knee in Dagenham 1932

Street, West Kensington, London. I was born in Dagenham, Essex on 22nd August 1932. My parents had moved to Dagenham to find work perhaps during the Great Depression (1929–1933); Ford had opened a new factory in Dagenham in 1931.

Charlie apparently didn't care for a little baby brother, attempting to bury me in the garden of 53, Ivinghoe Road, Dagenham. He did subsequently manage to squash my hand in the wooden rollers of a mangle (a machine used for pressing water out of newly washed clothes) – a squashed middle finger on my right hand is proof!

An interesting fact is why I, a Gentile boy, was circumcised, either at home or in hospital, is a mystery. Why my parents agreed (my brother wasn't) or what influenced them I am agnostic about. That I received the meaningful sign is indisputable, though I was in my sixties before I fully appreciated the fact! Psalm 16:11 says, 'You make known to me the path of life; you will fill me with joy in your presence, with eternal pleasures at your right hand' so perhaps from eight days old I was being prepared for my walk on the breakwater!

Dagenham was home for a short period, perhaps two or three years, before we returned to live at 47, Faroe Road, West Kensington, London. Its plot of ground was purchased by one Robert Spurway of High Street Fulham on 9th October 1854. He was a carpenter and 'erected a dwelling house upon the said plot of land which is known as Number 47 Faroe Road'.[2] He had a son, Robert, and three daughters: Emily, Rose and Kate. He died on 16th November 1898 (the year my father was born). My father bought the house in 1963 for £600 and we sold it for £20,000 in 1980.

Faroe Road (with Ceylon Road was possibly named after the Islands) was an inauspicious road situated in the Borough of Hammersmith or the Royal Borough of Kensington. The street is full of memories of the years 1936–1947. In the 30s and 40s the street was one long clear playground, no cars parked in those days so space was abundant. (Today, 2019, expensive cars park bumper to bumper.) Back then we played hopscotch, whip-and-top, marbles (rolled along the gutter), cowboys-and-Indians, or cops-and-robbers with ten or twelve boys and girls all happily together, disturbed only by deliveries of coal or milk from the horse-drawn carts. The occasional collapse of a shire horse within its shafts created great interest. Each evening the gas lamps ignited with a 'plop' as the lamplighter's long pole released gas into the bracket of the four or so lamps in the road.

Playing in the street could be hazardous at times; a home-made bow loosed an arrow which hit me in the left ear; a top from a whip-and-top broke a neighbour's window and Dad had to replace the broken pane.

The House

The house in Faroe Road still stands, now with an extra storey. Originally a Victorian eight-roomed house with sub-basement scullery, complete with coal-fired boiler and mangle for the weekly wash. And an outside toilet.

47 Faroe Road, my London home

The mangle squish-squashed water from freshly washed clothes. My brother attempted to mangle my two-year-old hand – to this day the third finger of my right hand bears the scar. He'd also tried to bury me in the garden of our home in Ivinghoe Road, Dagenham where I was born; was it jealousy? But through life we enjoyed a good relationship until the day he died in Carmarthen in 2003.

The house had no indoor bathroom so we went to an outhouse in the garden for the toilet. This was standard procedure proving an embarrassment years later when a girlfriend from work visited me at home (I was recovering from pleurisy) and asked mother for the toilet! Toilet paper didn't come in rolls; torn-up pieces of newspaper – *The Mirror* or *Daily Express* – hung on a nail inside the toilet door. At night-time we didn't go out to the toilet but used a chamber pot (a big pot with a handle), which was hidden under the bed. It was sometimes known as a 'Guzzunder' (because it 'goes under' the bed!).

I visited the old home in Faroe Road in September 2014 – it was fascinating. The present owners (who bought the house in 1980) have made alterations; a bathroom with shower is where the old kitchen used to be. An extra storey adorns the old roof space. The front first-floor bedroom (where coffins were laid out) is now a large lounge incorporating the middle bedroom (my cousin Barbara's). My old bedroom, which Charlie had turned into a bathroom for our mother, is now a book-lined study. Downstairs a wall has been removed allowing open space for a dining room. The old scullery and outside loo are now the breakfast room, and the basement entrance doorway transformed into a toilet.

Faroe Road, London W14 is not as remembered. The gas lamps have gone; two-storey houses have become three- or four-storey ones. Street-level properties now have basements; trees are planted and expensive cars park bumper to bumper. You couldn't play marbles in the gutter any more nor look for milk or coal being delivered by horse-drawn vehicles.

The Family

Life in Faroe Road was happy and contented. Two families lived there: the O'Brien's on the top half and the Cullen's in the bottom half. My father and Doris Cullen were brother and sister.

My mother, Kate Ellen Russell (interestingly Russells on both sides of the family), was born in Eccles, a lovely village in Kent. She was one of six children. Her father, a journeyman bricklayer, sadly was given to drink. I never knew him but his widow Grandma Russell lived at Number 47 for some time. Her room was a cosy bolt hole, coal fire blazing in the grate, a large five-draw chest of drawers, marble-topped washstand with ewer and basin by the window, bed and armchair

On my Grandmother's lap, with Mother and Charlie

furnished the room. A few photographs show her proudly standing with her grandsons, an erect woman with a firm countenance; only a few memories of her remain. She died whilst Charlie and I were away in Cornwall as evacuees.

Grandpa O'Brien lived with the Cullens. In retirement sitting on a chair at the top of the basement steps, smoking his clay pipe and greeting people who passed by. It was a happy household arrangement.

Mum and Dad on their wedding day

My parents Kate Ellen O'Brien (née Russell) and Charles John O'Brien had met in a local pub – either 'The Freemason's Arms' or 'The Parr's Head' (both located in Blythe Road W14) – during the 1920s. Mother was a barmaid and Dad a regular. They married at St Matthew's Church, Sinclair Road on 16th October 1927 when Dad was 29 and Mum 25.

Both parents came from large families with six or seven siblings so we had plenty of aunts and uncles. Doris, Dad's sister, lived downstairs at Number 47. She married Harry Cullen, a motor mechanic who became a postman. Their two children, Barbara and Reg, our two cousins, were useful playmates to have as we joined ten or twelve other children to play games.

Cousin Barbara died in 2012; we had last met in Stratton in 1999 when Charlie and I took a service at the Methodist church.

Auntie Phoebe, another sister, lived in the adjacent road; her husband was special to us for he was a London Underground train driver. Though we would occasionally see him in the driver's cab as we waited on the Hammersmith Underground platform, we never got to ride up front with him. Ivy, another of Dad's sisters, also lived nearby.

The Home

The kitchen was our main living room. There was an open fireplace with a blazing fire during the winter months – no central heating in the 1940s. A gas mantle on the right-hand wall was the only light until electricity was laid on. The kitchen housed a wooden table with four chairs, a dresser which held crockery, glasses, cutlery and food – we used to help ourselves to spoonfuls of Nestlé's milk from the opened tin! – a gas stove on the left next to the sink with only a cold-water tap; hot water came from a kettle or saucepans on the gas stove. The gas supply came from a meter on the landing outside the kitchen; penny coins (larger than the 1p coins we have now) were inserted into the meter to pay for the gas. Every once in a while (monthly) a gasman would call to empty the gas meter, taking the coin box out of the meter and emptying the coins onto the kitchen table, counting them into piles of twelve (one shilling) – we had pounds, shillings and pence in those days: twelve pence to a shilling and twenty shillings to the pound. He would bag them up I think five shillings to a bag. Over a certain amount meant a welcome rebate of a shilling or two.

Coal was delivered by black-faced, leather-clad coalmen who tipped sacks of coal through holes in the pavement, having first removed the round metal plates, into the cellar below. Seeing this activity was always a pleasure. Our coal, however, was carried down the basement steps, along the basement passage and shot into the space beneath the stairs. 'Getting the coal' meant carrying an empty scuttle down two flights of stairs and along two passages, filling it from the store beneath the stairs and returning to the kitchen/living room-cum-bathroom. It was where we listened to the Relay wireless, ate, washed, shaved and had our weekly bath.

We did all our washing in the kitchen, standing by the window. Water was heated in a kettle on the gas stove and poured into a basin in the sink. Father shaved there too (as we did when we grew older). He used a cutthroat razor which he honed on a leather strap hanging by the window. An oval-shaped mirror (now in our Stafford home), hung above the fireplace; it has seen the youthful images and Brylcreemed hair of growing teenagers.

Mum did all the cooking, mainly meat and two veg, but also Pease pudding, tripe and onions, soup and dumplings were provided, as well as bacon and eggs; we enjoyed our meals.

Ice-cream and shellfish sellers came to our front doors in pedal-driven or hand-pushed carts. Sunday-afternoon tea was frequently winkles, cockles or mussels purchased from the fishmonger's cart. A pin took the scab off the winkle, deposited it on the outer shell and the tasty curly winkle hooked out, eaten with bread and butter. A popular song of the day was about the man who had bought himself 'a penn'orth of winkles' only to find that 'his wife and her seven kids' were 'picking all the big-uns out'.

Unlike today with a constant supply of poultry, Christmas was anticipated with the one chicken each year to celebrate the Yuletide season.

Charlie and I shared the same bed. A very lumpy flock mattress. Having no bathroom, we had a weekly wash every Saturday evening in a large tin bath in front of the kitchen fire. Bath water was heated in kettles and saucepans on the gas stove. One of us would bath first and then the other would get into the bath, add some more hot water, and wash! Our parents also used to bathe like this.

As teenagers we went to public baths in Shepherd's Bush – a two-mile walk each way. The building was situated opposite the BBC radio offices. The baths were ideal and spacious; you shouted out, 'More hot water in number ten, please,' and the attendant would turn the tap on outside your cubicle so that hot water would gush into your bath. 'Thank you,' was shouted when enough hot water arrived.

Our parents, having met each other in a pub, it became part of their social life to continue visiting them. A regular Sunday-afternoon walk would take us along Blythe Road where the Post Office Savings Bank was situated, past The Olympia, along Kensington High Street, John Lewis and Debenhams. Going into Green Park, to the round pond, watching amateur yachtsmen sail their model boats. Alternatively, turning into Holland Walk and locating a pub in a side street. Mum and Dad went inside (children were not allowed, we waited patiently until Dad brought us out a glass of ginger beer and a packet of crisps). The total walk of some five or six miles still holds pleasant memories.

My Mother

My mother was born in Eccles, a Kent village. She was the youngest of seven children. I knew all my six aunts and uncles save one, Jack, who was killed in the First World War.

Harry and George, two uncles, visited us regularly; they both lived near Eccles. Being able gardeners, their visits to 47, Faroe Road brought home-grown vegetables – the fruit of their labours – which were always gladly received. Uncle Harry lived in Lunsford Lane; my cousins Barbara and Gavin are remembered. Gavin gave me a copy of *Scouting for Boys* long before scouting became a significant influence in my life.

Uncle Harry worked at Reed's paper mills and was a member of the local fire brigade. Tragically he was crushed to death whilst working on the huge rolls of newsprint paper. An early memory is seeing his coffin topped with his magnificent helmet laid upon a gleaming bright red and polished brass fire engine, which conveyed his body to church.

We travelled on the Green Line buses to Lunsford Lane to go hop picking. Londoners did this regularly to earn money. Hops grew very high, like runner beans, and had to be picked, collected in large containers, and weighed by the grower, then money given to the industrious day-long worker.

Uncle Fred had married May who was the widow of his dead brother Jack (Jack was killed on 4th July 1917 in France). Connie, their daughter, died in 2017. We regularly visited the family in Rayner's Lane. Herb, another brother, lived in New Hythe and his daughter Jean, another cousin, is still in touch. Visiting mother's sister Elsie involved crossing the river down by Reed's paper mill. My recollection is of a rather small dinghy rowed across a dark, forbidding mass of water, then a walk to 4, Victoria Street, Eccles – the cosy, warm yet unpretentious cottage where my mother was reared. During one visit to the local park we helped to fill sandbags which were to become air-raid shelters and barriers against enemy attacks and the threat of shrapnel.

Of the numerous cousins only Dennis Russell (Uncle George's son) and Jean (Uncle Herb's daughter) are in touch in 2019. These are all on my mother's side. My childhood memories of aunts and uncles on both sides of the family are happy and fulfilling.

My Father

I discovered that my father was conceived out of wedlock being born in September 1898 whilst his parents Charles William O'Brien (aged twenty-two) and Phoebe Amelia Russell (aged twenty) married in April 1898. His mother died aged thirty-five when my father was fifteen.

Dad was a tall, slim man who walked with a roll reminiscent of a sailor's gait on board ship. He had an equable character; I never saw him angry or ever heard him swear, although we frustrated him by not being quiet when going to bed, and he would come into our bedroom and whack the bed covers with his belt and tell us to go to sleep.

On my father's side there were six siblings in the family: Dad was the eldest followed by John, Edward, Phoebe, Ivy and Doris. I have memories of them all. Ted with his cheeky swagger and generous spirit (he once gave Charlie and me a sixpence each). Sadly he had a reputation of shady horse betting. He went to prison for stealing a bookmaker's bag.

Uncle John emigrated to Australia, returning once with a genuine Aboriginal boomerang which was tried out on the vicarage lawn in Doxey many years later with little success.

As I think back upon my childhood and my parents I am full of admiration for my father, though to my shame I once thought them inferior. A letter to Mary in 1960 expresses feelings of inferiority of my working-class background. Today, as I write this, an immense pride stirs my soul as I consider the parents God gave me. My father at fifteen, the eldest of six children, lost his mother and must have taken on a lot of responsibility for his younger brothers and sisters. At eighteen he was enlisted in the Royal Navy, on board HMS *Pembroke* and HMS *Sentinel* from 14th February 1917 to 23rd June 1919. He became an expert boiler fitter engineer, working with four-inch diameter cast iron piping, not the lightweight copper piping of today. He could wipe solder joints, repair boots and shoes, sitting with the three sole shaped heavy metal last between his knees, mouth full of brads, hammering them into the leather soles and heels of our boots. Metal Blakey's around the toes and heel edges would save wear and tear, though they made a clattering noise as we walked and played. He was an excellent decorator, using flour-and-water paste and stippling patterns with emulsion paint using a sponge. He repaired the roof using a sliding lead nail cutter to replace broken slates, and would sweep the chimney of soot when needed.

My Dad the Sailor

He was a very good workman; his father, my grandfather, was a portmanteau (case) maker working in leather, like his father before him. My mother's father was a bricklayer, so I've inherited some of their genes as a DIY'er.

We never discussed emotional, profound matters; I don't recall him ever speaking about his mother's death or childhood. A 'Present from Malta' picture of him as a sailor hung on the bedroom wall. He was a quiet, consistent, level-headed gentle man, not given to overt expressions of emotion although I recall his non-committal emotional silence when visiting me in Highwood Hospital in 1947.

One Saturday morning he took me to the Elephant and Castle Rowton House hostel where he worked. I have memories of him inside repairing a huge water boiler in the laundry, the ladies making a fuss of me with iced buns and lemonade. One final memory in 1963, whilst home from theological college because he was ill, I gave him a bed bath for his comfort. He died in Du Cane Road Hospital in 1963. May he rest in peace.

School Days

My earliest recollection is walking with my mother to nearby Addison Gardens Primary School (1936–1940), where my brother Charlie went. He, being older, was in another class. School days were happily spent colouring, painting, playing in the mobile sandpit wheeled into the classroom. The obligatory third-sized bottle of milk was collected from the crate in the cloakroom. In the first year we rested each day, going to the hall and lying on a camp bed for a while, and had a daily spoonful of sweet and tasty malt.

I particularly remember a break time in the playground one day sitting quietly forlorn as I dried out having peed myself, making the teacher wonder where 'this pool of water came from' on the classroom floor!

I also remember carrying home the Coronation mug celebrating the accession of King George VI and Queen Elizabeth in 1936, walking along Redan Street turning into Masbro Road, which ran parallel to Faroe Road where I lived.

Reading books has been a joy all my life; a junior school memory is of being so engrossed reading, head in hands at the back of the class, unaware that the whole class was looking and waiting expectantly for me to respond to the teacher's, 'Class, put your books away now.'

But school days became affected by the declaration of the Second World War. Prime Minister Neville Chamberlain on 3rd September 1939 announced, 'This country is at war with Germany.' Little did we know then that we would soon see and walk on the breakwater. We became 'evacuees'.

....

[2] Indenture of Purchase 4th April 1899

CHAPTER 2

Evacuation 1940–1943

On first seeing and walking on the breakwater.

....

Shortly after the outbreak of war in 1939 the British government advised families to send their children away to safer places. I have no clear recollection of being told that we were going away. No remembrance of crying or saying we didn't want to leave home – we accepted the fact. We had been through the beginnings of preparations for war. Windows of each room were crisscrossed with strips of sticky brown paper as a precaution against flying broken glass caused by any bomb blast.

Over two million 'Anderson shelters' (sectional steel shelters) were issued free to families. We had one in our garden; a deep hole was dug and a concrete base made; walls and roofs of steel covered with soil from the hole made the tent-like structure. I tore a hole in a new pair of shorts sitting astride the entrance corner of steel. During air raids – notified by the loud wailing sound of the air-raid siren – we moved down into the shelter and listened to the sound of aircraft and the 'womffph' 'womffph' of the 'ack-ack' guns, then the swishing sound of bombs coming down. Later on, during the V-1 flying bomb raids in 1944 ('V' was *'vergeltung'* – 'vengeance') these crafts, called doodlebugs, snarled across the sky, coughed, then silence . . . followed by a shattering explosion. I was playing in the street on Sunday 16th July 1944 when a V-1 demolished St Mary's Church on the corner of Edith Road.

Anderson shelters with their steel construction, covered with soil provided a measure of security for family members. We stayed there until the 'all clear' sounded. In the morning we would go off to school and look in the road or gutter for pieces of shrapnel, metal bits from exploding shells, which had fallen down.

It seemed sensible that children should be sent to safer places and so my brother Charlie and I were among several hundred London evacuees who went away in September 1940, our few meagre belongings carried in pillowcases, gas masks in brown cardboard boxes slung over shoulders. A coach at Edith Road took us with our cousin Barbara and other children to Waterloo Station. We boarded the London South Western Railway (LSWR) steam train for a journey of over five hours. Two hundred miles seemed tedious.

'Where are we going, Miss?' This to one of the accompanying teachers.

'Down there,' pointing out Bude on the compartment map above our heads.

'When will we get there?'

'Not very long now; behave yourselves and I'll see you later – you're not the only ones on this train you know.'

Arriving at Bude station in the dark we were transported to Bude Methodist church hall by the Strand and given refreshments.

Some of the children were billeted in Bude; we, with others, went to nearby Stratton, a market town some two miles inland. Another Methodist church hall saw us scrutinised and allocated to foster parents. Cousin Barbara was housed with a local grocer, Mr May, with his wife and their daughter Pam. Besides owning a grocery shop Mr May was a local returning officer. He also played the last post on a trumpet at the village war memorial on Remembrance Day. Twenty years later in 1962 on our honeymoon he drove us for an outing to Tintagel.

A young mother with two girls took in two young boys from London. Housed in a flat above a shoe shop in the main street just along from the bridge over the River Strat, we began our life as evacuees. The food was meagre; we larked about with the girls whilst the lady was out. We didn't stay there long. Our health deteriorated and the young mother, whose husband had been called to military service, found it too much. We were to be rehoused.

She found us paddling in the River Strat. 'Come along, I'm taking you both to your new home.' Mrs Curtis, as she was then ('Auntie Evelyn' later), was the housing officer for evacuees from London. 'You'll have to behave. Bill Davey is an ex-policeman from Plymouth and won't stand any nonsense!'

The admonition was appropriate as on the day we moved we had been playing in the water. The short journey from the River Strat to 'Hamvale', the Daveys' home, was made and two bedraggled boys, water dripping from their boots, arrived at the front door. Bill Davey and his wife met us. We promised never to go fishing again in our boots in the River Strat!

So began a lifelong relationship (walk) with two godly Methodist people, lasting until their deaths in the mid-1950s. Their influence is ongoing and eternal; a momentous decision with a lasting effect upon two urchin boys from west London. In many ways, experiences of those 1940s days helped mould our social skills, independence, usefulness, and laid a foundation of Christian faith. We learned to play whist with neighbours in 'Penryth', the next-door bungalow. Aunty and Uncle introduced us to various friends in Stratton: the Hockings owned a store near the chapel where their grown-up daughter sang in the choir and played the organ. We were invited to tea. Unfortunately the rich cream tea and chocolate biscuits made us give off some unpleasant odours whilst playing carpet bowls on the floor!

Market day saw herds of cattle crowding and mooing along the road, passing Hamvale on the way to be sold or slaughtered.

Uncle Bill and Auntie Flo, as we called them, lived in Hamvale, a bungalow sited on Hill Head ('Ham' being Florence's maiden name). They were in their sixties with no children of their own, having been prevailed upon by Mrs Curtis (a niece) to have two boys, Charlie and George O'Brien.

What must it have been for them to suddenly have the responsibility of caring for two young boys? How did they feel about two strangers entering their home? Did they have any experience of children? These are questions left unanswered yet we seemed to blend, melded together; perhaps their Christian social Methodist views conditioned any apprehensions they might have.

We were fed and watered; the abiding memory of that first day was after having a bath – *in a proper bathroom not in a tin bath by the fire* – we were transported, being carried on Uncle Bill's shoulders from the bathroom to our bed and dumped into the enveloping heap of a feather bed. What a revelation this was, miles away from the lumpy flock mattress in London. Our New Home was a place of comfort and security.

It was an exciting life for two London 'urchins' who'd played hopscotch and 'tin can copper' in London's streets to discover the joys of life in the country. We settled into a new family life at Hamvale, helping Uncle in the garden, cutting the front roadside hedge with sheep-shearing clippers. A large red postman's bike became a play item and the local blacksmith neighbour made two metal hoops for us to roll with short lengths of wood along the largely traffic-free roads. We graduated to large motor car tyres which were more difficult to handle but great fun to trundle along the main road and around the local nearby country lanes.

We became familiar with Jordan's Hill Head Farm through collecting our milk from Farmer Jordan's cows; the milk poured into a jug, often still warm, having come direct from the cow. We wanted to see how the milk came into the bucket and so had our experience of sitting at the rear end of the cow – she tethered at the eating trough and giving a quizzical look behind when feeling the inexperienced hands trying to pull and squeeze teats at the same time to make a jet of milk hit the side of the bucket with a 'fizz dunk' every time.

We went searching in the hedgerows for chickens' eggs; chased rabbits escaping from the combine harvester in the cornfields. Haymaking, bringing the cows in for milking and mucking out were all activities we did on the farm. We learnt about life too – how the bull mounted the cow, how piglets came into the world and lambs were born in the field; also how male lambs were 'knackered' (or castrated) and, more traumatically, how a particular farmhand took more than a passing fancy to little boys in the back of the shippens!

Starling pie is very tasty – made after the birds had been plucked and lead pellets removed. Farmer Jordan's double-barrelled shotgun had decimated them after they had been enticed down to the corn seed in the farmyard. Perhaps the most enduring memory of those days on the farm was witnessing the 'sticking' of a large sow hauled up by the ring in her snout to the lintel of the shippen door and despatched with shrill shrieks and pouring blood from the severed throat. The head, trotters and intestines were duly carried in a tin bath back to Hamvale where Aunty Flo made brawn from the head and trotters, and 'hogs puddings' (sausages) from the intestines (duly cleaned and washed out) and chitterlings – made from the small intestine. In September we would go blackberry picking armed with baskets and old umbrella sticks which had a curved handle to pull down the high brambles. We would walk for miles and be away hours searching for and picking blackberries. There was no fear of getting lost or abducted in those days. It was great fun finding daffodils, bluebells and primroses growing in the fields and taking bunches home; it seemed all right to do so – not thought of as stealing. On the other hand, scrumping (taking apples from Farmer Jordan's orchard) wasn't right. We once got caught and Uncle was informed – can't remember the outcome! Hamvale became a place of utter, absolute security.

The four strangers – an elderly married, childless couple and two London streetwise kids – blended together in a remarkable way. The only photograph reveals a beautiful foursome. Proud foster parents, with two young immaculately attired bright-eyed, chubby cheeked boys.

With hindsight, how we developed a relationship with Uncle Bill and Auntie Flo is difficult to assess. The overwhelming remembrance is one of complete and utter trust, contentment and enjoyment. They, in their late sixties, married for forty years but childless, took to adoption with complete ease. We became known as 'Bill Davey's little boys'.

A glass-fronted bureau in the living/dining room contained a Toby Jug:

There are friends and friends,
Kind folk we meet in passing on our way,
Who cheer us with a happy smile
Or something that they say.
Friends too who know us in our varied spheres,
Comrades at play or colleagues through the years,
We all have many such, but ah how few,
Are blessed as I am with friends like you.

Memorised as an eight-year-old evacuee boy, it's a lovely reminder of that comfortable home and wonderful foster parents.

Another item of pottery had the rhyme:

Within this jug there is good liquor
Fit for Parson and for Vicar
But how to drink and not to spill
Will test the utmost of your skill

Trying to drink from the jug was impossible; you were drenched with water as you lifted the jug to your mouth. The secret was having a finger covering a small hole beneath the jug's handle.

I have always enjoyed poetry; perhaps seeing and memorising those Toby Jug verses set a trend. Years later 'The Seven Ages of Man' from *As You Like It* was also learnt by heart. The sequence from the 'infant mewling and puking in the nurses arms' to that 'last scene of all that ends this strange eventful history' indicates a whole range of relationships. Now in my eighties I'm nearer to 'that last scene' which awaits everyone and I look forward to it with great anticipation. Sheldon Vanauken (1914–1996), who was a professor of English at Oxford University, in *Under the Mercy* writes, 'And death if our faith does not fail is the great adventure.'[3] Death for me has become a great anticipated adventure because of that deeper profound 'walk' with Almighty God which Psalm 139 declares, 'You discern my going out and my lying down; you are familiar with all my ways . . . For you created my inmost being; you knit me together in my mother's womb . . . I am fearfully and wonderfully made.'

These memoirs indicate many varied relationships which have fashioned me. It has been fascinating to look back and wonder at the relationships which have developed; of course 'we all have many such' it's part of the rich tapestry of life. Yet there are special and unique ones to each individual, which make us the person we are.

Rationing in Cornwall seemed remote. Food seemed plentiful. Cornish pasties still make the juices run in my eighties. Auntie was expert at making pasties – she was an excellent cook. Watching her roll out pastry, loading large slaps of butter or lard onto it, spreading it liberally, dicing the potatoes and beef skirt contents, folding and crimping the pastry, forming each individual-looking pasty coated with milk and egg, baked golden brown. We each had a big one made from meat and potato and sometimes with an egg, all cooked inside golden crusty pastry. Devoured eagerly, even at times with liberal amounts of fresh full-cream milk!

Roast dinners, junkets, memories of that newly slaughtered pig's head, trotters and intestines carried from the farmyard in a tin bath and turned into delicious brawn, hogs puddings and chitterlings are still fresh decades later. She also taught us how to skin a rabbit.

Christmas meant going to a local farm for a goose, prepared for cooking not in the gas oven but in the range in the dining room, specially opened up for the occasion. Interestingly I have no recollection of getting presents. Did our parents send any from London? It's a real blank.

Auntie was also an excellent knitter: socks, gloves, pullovers were turned out in record time as she sat in her corner armchair, a third knitting needle housed in a wooden frame tucked under her arm. The 'Dedication' picture reveals how we looked with knitted pullovers and long socks.

'Uncle Bill', William Davey born in Byton in the 1890s, was a retired Devon policeman. At six-feet tall he was a big-framed man with large hands and could wield a truncheon with good effect, being more than a match for the matelots of the Devon shipyards on leave, worse for wear after too much drink. We would sit on each arm of his large comfortable armchair, snuggled into his broad shoulders as he regaled us with stories of his service days as a Plymouth policeman. An ongoing part of his police training was to boot-polish our boots with his and polish the underneath instep between sole and heel. Each Sunday morning he would take a large brush on his shoulders, walk down the hill to the Stratton playing field and sweep the shelter of any rubbish left there. He tended the garden, growing vegetables and flowers. And we helped, picking runner beans and helping make the winter potato store, a straw igloo structure covered with soil to protect the vegetables from frost. To this day my appreciation of primroses and lily of the valley comes from those growing in the garden of Hamvale, and recall those days eighty years ago.

The war appeared rather remote from our Bude perspective. Uncle did 'Night Watch' duty in the hut situated at the top of Downscote View. Very little happened; occasional convoys crossing the Atlantic horizon would be studied through binoculars from Hamvale's windows. But when Plymouth was bombed relatives came for some respite. A stick of bombs dropped in a field from a returning German plane was the maximum we had. The local 'Dad's Army' Home Guard trained in Stratton with rifle practice off the Big Hill leading to Hillhead.

Hamvale bungalow provided a view of the Atlantic Ocean with the outline of convoys sailing past. It was in Bude that my 'walk on the breakwater' came closer. Picnics on Summerleaze Beach gave us our first view of the breakwater. Summerleaze Beach, a magnificent area of golden sand with a well-made sea pool fashioned and constructed in 1929, is part of Bude's historic landscape. I learnt to swim in that pool, experiencing great satisfaction on reaching the far side of the deepest part. On the breakwater is 'Tommy's Pit' built into the breakwater by Sir Thomas Acland; this was Bude's first swimming pool before the sea pool on Summerleaze Beach was built. Tommy's Pit affords a pleasant dip. Children and adults enjoy jumping into the pit at the deep end. Also on the breakwater is Chapel Rock, thought to date to when Bude was 'really just a chapel on a rock'. Good views are obtained if you climb to the top.

In London our schooling had become ragged: teachers were called up for military service, school days had irregular hours. With other evacuees we attended the local school in Stratton, then moved to the Lecture Hall. We had periods of sitting with our gas masks on to get used to them in case of emergency. Miss Thomas, our teacher, was responsible for our welfare. She took a particular interest in my brother Charlie who developed rheumatic fever; she would rub coal tar oil into his arms each day. When we turned eleven we moved to the 'New School' nearer to Hill Head. An abiding memory there is hearing Mendelssohn's *Fingal's Cave* for the first time.

Postcard from Stratton 1942

Auntie Doris, Barbara's mother from Faroe Road, visited Stratton in July 1942. A postcard home says, 'The boys are fine – I'm taking them to the beach this afternoon.' Our own parents also came for a holiday. We went by hired car to Bude station where we joyfully met them. They were tickled by our Cornish accents and expressions.

Christian Values

Above and beyond the comfort and security of Hamvale was the abiding Christian faith we were introduced to. Good Methodist believers, each Sunday evening we walked two miles with Uncle Bill and Auntie Flo to Bush Chapel, greeting friends and neighbours en route. Stairs to the balcony area gave access to the 'Daveys' pew'. We enjoyed singing from the Methodist hymnbook. Favourite hymns included 'Will Your Anchor Hold in the Storms of Life', 'Pass Me Not,

Outside Stratton Methodist Church with Charlie and Cousin Barbara 1999

O Gentle Saviour' and 'In Lovingkindness Jesus Came'. Uncle Bill had a deep base voice. 'We have an anchor which keeps the soul, steadfast and sure while the billows roll' resounded throughout the building.

Sunday school at Stratton Methodist Chapel, morning and afternoon, became a regular discipline earning us prizes for full attendance. My Methodist hymnbook prize dated April 1941 is falling apart from good use. To those days belong the faithful ministry of Miss Clough, Sunday school teacher who taught us 'Jesus loves me, this I know for the Bible tells me so'. After my earthly walk is over one of the joys of eternity will be to worship our Saviour with Miss Clough, and to thank her for her faithfulness.

Evacuation for us was very good. We were away for some two-and-a-half years. Auntie regularly sent homemade Cornish pasties to us. Stratton and Bude are continuing memories. Over the years we have holidayed there and 'Going for a walk on the breakwater' has become an aphorism for doing something different and exciting – I also entertain a wish, should I die and be cremated, that my ashes might one day be scattered over the breakwater!

Evacuation eventually ended, we returned home to London but we never lost touch with Uncle Bill and Auntie Flo. In 1947 I spent some convalescence with them after having had pleurisy. We attended their funerals in 1954 and 1956.
....

[3]Sheldon Vanauken, *Under the Mercy* (Ignatius Press 1988)

CHAPTER 3

Return to London

O walk with Jesus, wouldst thou know
How deep, how wide His love can flow!
They only fail His love to prove
Who in the ways of sinners rove.[4]

• • • • • • •

Evacuation for us finished and we returned to take up life in London again. It's fascinating that I have no memory of leaving Auntie and Uncle; no memory of a tearful 'Goodbye' or how we travelled to Bude station, or whether Mother was with us on the journey home. There is one recollection of walking home from Hammersmith Underground Station to Faroe Road along Caithness Road, turning into Blythe Road to see the devastation caused by the land mine which exploded on the shops.

We returned home before the war ended and found the streets nearby very damaged by German bombs. Damage was caused to our house; the kitchen wall had a bulge in it. Dad bought the house for the princely sum of £600 in 1963. The wall was eventually repaired in 1970.

We both returned to school. Charlie started work as an electrician in Shepherd's Bush; I think he left school at age fourteen. He was conscripted for National Service at eighteen and stayed in till he was twenty. He was in the Royal Electrical Mechanical Engineers (REME) but never went abroad. After the army he started at Rowton House hostels and went to night school to qualify as an electrician, starting as an electrician's mate working with Ernie the electrician. Rowton House hostels was where Dad worked, who helped get him the job. Charlie I think stayed at Rowton's for thirty-five years and then moved to Ealing Hospital. The hospital was trying to reduce costs and doubled his pension years if he left, so he did. Later on he worked at EMI, finishing his working life at Brunel University aged sixty-five.

In due course he met Eileen Best and they were married at St Mary's Church hall in North End Road with the wedding breakfast at 47, Faroe Road. I was Charlie's best man. Charlie and Eileen were blessed with four daughters: Sue, Julie, Lynn and Helen, with Martin, Nick, Steve and grandchildren Darren, Michael, Robert, Rachel and Matthew.

I returned to Addison Gardens Junior School then moved to West Kensington Central Secondary School, situated in Fulham Palace Road; the Number 11 bus from Brook Green, a short walk from Faroe Road, took me there. I sat next to Margaret Simpson at the back of the class. Jack Davey, Robert Ben-Nathan (known as Bob) and Alan Shillingford became firm friends. Bob and Alan are still in touch in 2019. I was getting poor marks in some subjects till it was discovered that I was short-sighted so moved to the front of the class. I eventually got glasses and recall the joy of being able to see more clearly. Fifty years later a similar experience occurred after cataract operations.

D-Day was declared on 6th June 1944. The Second World War ended in 1945.

School days were happy at Fulham Palace Road with most lessons being held there, although metal work was at another school where David Goldband's lock of curly black hair got yanked off in one of the machines! I made a metal door latch and sent it to Uncle Bill for his garden shed door. Woodwork was taught at FPR where I made a pencil box, a sandpaper knife-sharpener and started an ambitious rocking horse, which never got finished.

Sixth Form, 1949. I'm standing at the back by the lampost! Alan Shillingford on left second row. Bob Ben-Nathan seated front right with girl's hands on shoulders

School premises changed to nearer home and the Olympia, then to Lillie Road, where the French teacher's class became the Sixth Form. By then I had become a Prefect but Joe Deary pipped me to becoming Head Boy!

And then came a detour on my 'walk on the breakwater'.

During 1947 I became ill with pleurisy and was put on the TB register and monitored each year until removal from the register in 1963. I was admitted to Du Cane Road Hospital for treatment under the care of Dr A.V. Bird. The ward, a traditional Francis Nightingale one with fifteen to twenty beds each side of a long room; the nursing station was a desk just inside the door with Sister's office at the entrance.

Treatment consisted of draining fluid from my right lung by a needle being inserted into the pleural cavity and drawing off the fluid through a tube attached to a syringe. Life in a ward full of older men was quite an experience; ribald comments and suggestive pictures were commonplace. Even the question from one of the doctors, 'When did you start to become a man?' was embarrassing. You learn a lot being in hospital. Attractive nurses in smart uniforms ministered to our various needs: serving food, bringing bedpans and bottles for our toilet needs and giving bed baths. Each evening patients scanned the ward entrance for a glimpse of ward visitors, family members eager to know how the patient was and presenting gifts of sweets, fruit and reading material. Various stages of illness were present and occasionally all bed curtains would be drawn whilst a deceased patient was removed from the ward. My stay lasted several weeks before being discharged.

Memories of Life in Highwood Hospital Brentwood

In 1947 I was scheduled for a period of convalescence in Highwood Hospital Brentwood, Essex that was to last for several months. The place and time are very significant both psychologically and ultimately spiritually for me. Experiences I had, people I met all played and continue to play a major part in my life.

Highwood Hospital consisted of a number of two-storey buildings called 'houses' within extensive grounds. Each house was named after a tree – The Beeches, The Oaks and The Rowans where I was. The ground floor had a number of cots with young babies from just a few months old; upstairs the rest of us young boys. At age fifteen I was one of the eldest. Bed rest was the accepted treatment for lung diseases, with plenty of fresh air and good food.

The winter of 1947 was a harsh one; in the convalescent home sleeping out in the open balcony allowed snow to blow in and lie on the bottom of the bed.

Meals were provided and clean clothing from the laundry facilities. 'Kate' in charge sized us up each week and provided the appropriate clean pyjamas, underwear, etc. Nursing staff in other similar buildings lived on site. The hospital superintendent – a qualified doctor – had his own residence which was a large detached house within the grounds.

Schooling was also important and local teachers visited the wards providing tuition. As we improved health-wise various forms of rehabilitation were provided. J.S. Pond, the local Scout District Commissioner, formed a Scout troop. Earning my tenderfoot badge I was invested as a Scout. Being one of the eldest I was immediately promoted to Patrol Leader with two white stripes adorning the left pocket of my uniform. Blue shirt, shorts and red neck scarf secured with a woggle made an attractive looking Patrol. My Patrol consisted of six boys, one of whom, Jim, and I slept in beds alongside each other; he hailed from Dulwich and was keen on boxing – he would write off and get autographed pictures of current boxers. After our discharge I visited him at his home in Dulwich. He was to become well known, even notorious; I will tell you more about him as we continue our journey along the breakwater.

Life in Highwood Hospital was to become very meaningful and influential with ongoing repercussions even to my late eighties. Life on the ward or in the house became a family affair; nursing staff cared for all male patients from young babies to teenagers. Sister Anita Bellevue was in charge; an Irish ex-Army Sister, she was a formidable person with a stentorian voice who kept ordered discipline.

She doted on me. After being allowed up from total bed rest, she treated me to the pictures in Brentwood, and then we had afternoon tea and a walk in the local park. I was overawed by her attention which went beyond the bounds of propriety. She subsequently visited me at home after my discharge.

Ten months were spent in Highwood Hospital. Celebrating Christmas 1947 was fun. Roy Rich, another patient, shared his large tin of chocolate biscuits around. Each patient had a personal metal bowl which contained his sweets and chocolates, these being distributed by the staff at appropriate times.

The annual summer garden fete was held in August. I won two prizes: the treasure hunt and handicrafts competition (a log cabin hut made from twigs gathered by staff from the grounds).

In the summer of 1948 I returned home to West Kensington and back to school in preparation for the School Leaving Certificate – an equivalent to Matriculation. Seven subjects were needed to qualify for a certificate.

My earlier schooling had been disrupted, first at junior school because of evacuation, then a missed year at Highwood Hospital. I sat the School Leaving Certificate in 1949 but failed to obtain seven subjects, passing in English, English Literature, History, with a credit in Art, not sufficient for a Certificate. The opportunity to re-sit in November was not taken up and I started out in working life.

I became an office boy in Ledgard's, a textile retail outlet located in Wigmore Street, London W2. Silmyra fabric was produced for the linings for Windsmoor coats. Ledgard's treated their employees well; we all received a brace of pheasants at Christmas and had summer coach trips to the seaside. Joan Orchard was the attractive receptionist; we went swimming occasionally – she was the first girl I kissed. She visited me in King George V Sanatorium in Godalming,

Surrey when I had a relapse of my TB. Another girl who lived near the Brompton Oratory was taken out to tea and to the pictures at the Odeon on Kensington High Street. She also visited me at home during my relapse. Nothing romantically developed, I never kissed her! I wonder what happened to them?

I continued my walk on the breakwater.

It's possible that my working life might have been in the rag trade – after working as the office boy I progressed to the warehouse where the rolls of material were checked in, measured and stamped with Ledgard's truth mark. Then onto the dyeing department where Mr King, a large-built friendly man, was the manager who was keen on ballet and where I first learnt about *pas de deux* and *entrechat*. It was in this department that I inadvertently spoilt several yards of rare Italian silk with an ink stain. It was only years later that I wrote and confessed my misdemeanour and received a gracious letter of acceptance and forgiveness. But the rag trade was not for me.

Having experienced the excitement of scouting at Highwood Hospital, in 1948 I was keen to continue. I enquired of Alan Shillingford, a classmate, which Scout troop he belonged to. He introduced me to the 10th Fulham (St Andrew's) Scout troop. Rumour had it that Fulham Football Club's early beginnings started at St Andrew's Church. I enjoyed six years of scouting as a Senior Sea Scout, Rover Scout

10th Fulham Senior Sea Scouts. I'm on the left. Alan Shillingford 3rd from right

and Assistant Scout Master. The friendship, enthusiasm, community and personal living ethics of scouting moulded my life. I remained in touch with Pat Talfourd and Eve Acres, 'Arkela' and 'Barloo' of the Cub Pack for many years. Eve died in 2017, Pat in July 2021.

Being prepared, doing a good deed a day and following the Scout Law became very meaningful. 'A Scout's duty is to honour the King', 'obey the Scout Law' and 'a Scout's word is to be trusted'. 'Trusty, loyal and helpful, brotherly, courteous kind, obedient, smiling and thrifty, clean in body and mind' summed up the Scout Law and became the framework for my life. A memorable incident as a sea scout, camping by the Solent, was when we were out in a small dinghy with a makeshift sail which drifted across the path of the paddle steamer ferry to the Isle of Wight. The paddle clanking sounds of the fast-approaching ferry encouraged us to 'out oars' and move out of danger. Back at camp we heard that the steamer captain, spotting our dilemma, ordered 'Dead slow ahead'!

But an even more momentous and significant event in my 'walk on the breakwater' was to happen. Andrew Forbat – a part-time Scout Master – fitted in visits to the troop from his work as a medical doctor. Andrew's roots were in a Hungarian Jewish family who immigrated to England in 1936. Andrew and John, his brother, had been through the troop and were now Scouters (leaders). Andrew had become a Christian believer through meeting Derrick Rose, another medical student, whilst in training. When I met him Andrew witnessed to his faith in Jesus Christ. He would speak to the young scouts and recommend reading the Bible. Copies of Scripture Union Bible Study Notes were given out. Andrew's enthusiastic questioning of the Bible passage was disconcerting because I did not then possess a Bible!

At Bagster's Bible Book Shop in Wigmore Street, along from Ledgard's where I worked, I purchased for ten shillings (50p) a flexible black-covered copy of the Authorised Bible. It was a strange feeling handling that Bible; with its clear onyx typeface perhaps I sensed unwittingly it would become important in my life.

I was a teenager going through the changes from puberty to young manhood. Emotions stirred in me and spiritual things were all part of my growing uncertainties, so when Andrew spoke to me about Christian belief I said, 'I've always been interested.' We arranged to meet on the 4th July 1949 at the Medical Mission where he worked as a locum in Upper Street, Islington.

July 4th 1949 was to become my spiritual birthday for in Andrew's room I knelt and hesitantly confessed my need and asked Christ to receive me. That incident was to have far-reaching consequences in my 'walk on the breakwater'. It laid the foundation of life-changing events, leading to local and international evangelism, youth work and open-air witness. Subsequently a green leaflet, a carol service invitation, led to marriage and a lifetime's work and ministry in the Church of England.

But first there was the Fulham and South Kensington YMCA (still an ongoing part of my life seventy years later). As a support to a young Christian, Andrew introduced me to Rob and Evelyn Maltby, the managers of a small boarding house for twenty-one men. 'Fairlawn', a large Victorian house, was situated at 643, Fulham Road. Designated a YMCA it was independent of the National Council and run as a lodging house for young men working and studying in London.

The Maltbys opened their home for communal meals and

friendship. After-church meetings were run on a Sunday evening, Bible studies mid-week and an early-morning prayer meeting at 7am on Sunday mornings. To this happy welcoming group I was introduced and a close bond of friendship developed. The Maltbys became my mentors and teachers in the Christian faith. A number of books in my library indicate their concern for my spiritual well-being. The Maltbys were Christian Brethren and worshipped at Churchgate Hall Assembly, alongside Putney Bridge, across the River Thames, near where the Boat Race starts. It was there that I received Christian baptism by full immersion on the 13th September 1951.

Where I was baptised by immersion, 13th September 1951

Part of the life at the YMCA was a Covenanter group – a Christian club for boys led by two schoolmasters David Owen and John Enstone. A regular Sunday-afternoon Bible class, seventy-plus in number, met at Fairlawn. Enthusiastic chorus singing conducted by David Owen was enjoyed by the boys. I was welcomed and subsequently became an assistant leader. Summer camps were held at West Runton, Norfolk and Cricieeth, Wales.

Dennis Lennon (1932-2016) one of the Covenanters became an O. M. missionary in Thailand, subsequently being ordained in the Church of England. A notable author writing Bible notes for Scripture Union with two books on prayer 'Turning the

Diamond' and 'Fueling the Fire' Anything from his pen is good measure!

I became very close to the Maltbys, helping in the hostel doing voluntary work, bookkeeping. In 1952 Rob Maltby invited me to work full time as an assistant to the secretary. I left Ledgard's to live-in and work at the YMCA, learning to administer a boarding house, dealing with accounts, cooking breakfast, cleaning the toilets and renovating the garden. And open-air preaching at meetings in North End Road, where a market was held each Saturday. A portable platform was set up and the Good News of Jesus was proclaimed.

Me preaching in North End Road, Fulham

Social occasions, parties with the ladies from the Earls Court YWCA were thoroughly enjoyed. In both hostels, invitations to give a testimony or lead the Sunday-morning prayer meeting were opportunities gladly taken. Local churches were visited. Dawes Road Baptist Church with their Pastor Andrew Kennedy. St. Matthew's Church, wandsworth Bridge Road, where Gary and Norma Piper worshipped; they were to become close friends.

One profound influence in my early Christian life was to be introduced to the ministry of Dr Martyn Lloyd-Jones, minister and great orator of Westminster Chapel in London. To sit under his preaching – an hour-long sermon, morning and evening for some two years – was a profound experience. It encouraged confidence to 'preach the Word'.

Life on this part of my walk was both a blessing and a pain. Through my own foolishness and indiscretion as a young twenty-year-old attracted to a pretty face – I thought I was 'in love' and made my feelings known but it was more sensual than spiritual – and in shame I left in May 1953. The committee minutes very sensitively recorded my departure. Stan Seymour, a trainee London City Missioner resident in the YM, gave me a book by Evan Hopkins, *The Law of Liberty in the Spiritual Life*, graciously inscribed with his appreciation of my work. F.B. Meyer, pastor and author, advises anyone 'to ask counsel at the mouth of the Lord' before entering into any relationship. He also says that God 'overrules our mistakes and brings blessing out of sins'.[5]

....

[4] Edwin Paxton Hood (1820–1885).

[5] FB Meyer *Joshua and the Land of Promise* (CLC Publications 2013) p.108

CHAPTER 4

Billy Graham Crusade, Harringay Arena. Bristol, Training for Ministry

Teach me Thy way, O Lord,
Teach me Thy way!
Thy gracious aid afford,
Teach me Thy way![6]

. . . .

In May 1953 I went back home to Faroe Road and fretted. For six weeks I was out of work, 'in the wilderness' as a Tax Inspector said many years later when scrutinising my tax records.

It was a time for realising that a walk on a breakwater can have its pitfalls: slippery stones and uneven places can make it a hazardous place. 'There has been more than one rescue from the breakwater in recent years.'[7] I was in the doldrums, feeling I'd let God down, disappointed the Maltbys and been unkind. 'When my heart is overwhelmed: lead me to the rock that is higher than I' (Psalm 61:2) spoke into my need during those six weeks. Andrew Forbat paid for a weekend at Hildenborough Hall (a Christian conference centre in Kent, run by Tom Rees). It was good to have Andrew's support and friendship. He was an anaesthetist and caused a chuckle amongst the conference members when he said, 'I put people to sleep.'

Tom Rees was a prominent evangelist and preacher who could fill the Royal Albert Hall for a Christian Mission.

Knowing that I needed work he recommended that I apply to the Evangelical Alliance. Preparations were being made for a Billy Graham Crusade at Harringay Arena in London.

The Campaign proper was scheduled to start on 1st March 1954. I started work at 19, Bedford Place working an addressograph machine, typing metal plates with names and addresses of supporters to receive postal information. Such was the interest that we worked through the night to get material ready for the post office delivery. Larger offices were needed because of the pressure of space at Bedford Place. City Gate House offices behind Holborn Underground Station were acquired. I moved there, learnt to 'mimeograph' and use a Gestetner duplicating machine, printing details of locations of 'nights of prayer' venues and information of counsellor training classes.

Charlie Riggs of the Billy Graham Team invited me to be his 'Andrew' assistant as he travelled giving counsellor training sessions in St Mary's Church, St Albans, in Ilford and Dawes Road Baptist Church Fulham. On one occasion, presented with a boiled egg for tea in a vicarage, he said with his slow American drawl, 'Say, how d'yer tackle this?'

The forthcoming mission found favour with a large number of churches of all denominations; many hundreds of people wanted to be involved, training as counsellors, choir members and stewards. A publicity film, *Oiltown USA*, was used to great effect portraying Billy Graham's missions in America.

Prayer was a vital preparation; individual prayer partners, prayer groups 'Cottage Prayer Meetings' were organised by Miss Ada Scarles and over five hundred groups were formed. All-night prayer meetings were a challenge; I went several times to St Paul's, Portman Square. A year's prayer preceded the twelve weeks of Mission.

It was exciting to be at the forefront of planning a major event with an international evangelist.

On Saturday 27th February a 'Dedication Service' was held in Harringay Arena for some five thousand workers (counsellors, office staff, stewards and other helpers). Billy Graham introduced team members and addressed the congregation. 'Then he did something which no one had expected and which he had not anticipated doing himself. He asked any who felt they were not right with God and wished to rededicate themselves to Christ, to leave their seats and stand in front of the platform.'[8] With another staff member I went out and prepared the counselling room seats with appropriate literature. Sixty-nine people came forward for counselling.

I attended most if not all of the nightly meetings at Harringay, allocating counsellor seating, counting the collection with the aid of a coin-sorting machine. I also trained as a counsellor and counselled ten people, over the years losing touch with all except one, David Barker, who is still in touch in 2019.

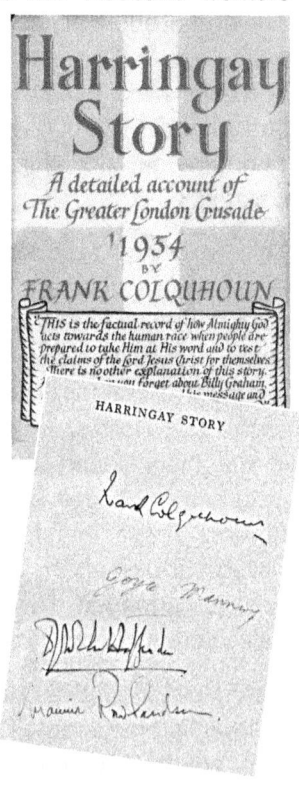

Account of Harringay Arena, Billy Graham Mission 1954 with Wilson-Haffenden's autograph

One particular memory, seated behind the choir one evening as Billy Graham gave the invitation and many people got out of their seats in response, is of noticing a woman weeping seated in front of me. I enquired if she wanted to go forward. A tear-laden face looked at me and said, 'I went forward last night.'

'Wonderful,' I replied and went down to the counselling room.

The overall attendances at Harringay during the twelve-week period reached an estimated figure of 1,756,000; recorded decisions were 36,431. The total cost of the campaign was budgeted at £100,000 which was exceeded by £48,000 but, with generous donations from America, all the costs were covered.

This exciting experience of Breakwater International Evangelism was to take a more significant turn. Working as a secretary Pauline Young (in name and age) was enthusiastic about personal witnessing. She, with her husband, Mike, formed 'The London Team'– a group of young Christians who each Bank Holiday would engage in evangelistic activities in the then County of Huntingdonshire, camping in the picturesque villages of Hemingford Grey and Hemingford Abbots. These enthusiasts, supported by local families, visited, preached, held outdoor meetings, took Sunday schools, arranged 'Rallies' on Saturday evenings with a visiting preacher or a 'Fact and Faith' film.

Mary Holman was secretary of the Hunts Young Peoples' Fellowship. Her parents, Dora and Aubrey Holman, supported. Mary attended team meetings in Hemingford Grey Chapel. She was to become very special on the breakwater of my life.

The Harringay Mission concluded. Billy Graham returned in 1955 for a mission in Scotland. And I became surplus to requirements. A Baptist minister working for the Evangelical

Alliance was concerned for my future. He took me out for an evening meal and prayed for God's will to be known in my life, wherever the walk on the breakwater would take me.

David Owen, one of the Covenanter leaders at the YMCA, knew that the Covenanter Union headquarters in City Gate House, Finsbury Square was looking for a bookkeeper and shop assistant. So following my redundancy I went to work for Covenanters, a new place of work and interest. In the event, I was to be there for some six years, working with Bill Dyer the shop manager. Laurie Withrington (Covenanters' General Secretary), his secretary Gill Jacobs and Mrs Preston made up the staff. Later Gerald Harris came to work in the office. He married Joy but sadly died at an early age; we're still in touch with his widow. Each Monday morning, the working week started with prayer as the staff stood together and committed the week to God.

It was fascinating working with a church-based Christian youth organisation. Covenanters came into being through a remarkable set of coincidences. Unknown to each other, two independent Christian men, Roland Webb in Wallington and John Cansdale in Rugby, with a desire to help young boys, both thought that Scottish Covenanters sounded exciting; they designed similar emblems and studies, and then discovered each other's existence and so formed 'The Covenanter Union'. In 1930, Capt. R.W. Pinchback (1892-2001) became Hon. Travelling Secretary. National rallies were held in Birmingham and London, and summer camps in West Runton, Norfolk and Criccieth, North Wales. One summer I spent six weeks under canvas on the Abbs Farm in West Runton, helping to staff three different camps either as 'Woody' doing camp-craft activities or as Adjutant. These camps were wonderful opportunities for relating to young boys. Fresh air, fun and games with youngsters from many parts of England; they making new friends and enjoying the bonhomie and evening marquee gatherings, with songs telling the old, old story of Jesus and His love. A lovely remembered conversation:

"Woody," (I taught camp-craft) said a boy to me at a Covenanter camp in 1959. "Woody, are you going to marry Cookie?" (Mary did the cooking.)

"Yes. Why?"

"Well you said you're twenty-seven – you might live until you're eighty."

We did!

Back at Covie headquarters in City Gate House, London another activity gripped me. Every Thursday lunch hour, by the fountain on the corner of Finsbury Square and City Road, an open-air meeting took place. London City Missioner Len Hodges started it. I joined the group of Christians proclaiming the gospel from a portable stand. We had many opportunities to speak with passers-by about faith, belief in God, Jesus Christ and our eternal destiny. An interesting account of the open-air meetings was published in *The Christian Herald* newspaper.

Finsbury Square Open Air Witness. Mary and me on the right.

Demolition and re-building of offices opposite the fountain across City Road went on apace. We prayed that other Christians would come to work there and support us. And thus I met up again with Mary Holman from Huntingdon. Little did I know then that in meeting Mary we would be walking on the same breakwater for over fifty-six years.

It was through a remarkable set of circumstances. I had given a month's notice to the Covenanters, believing I needed to earn more money to finance ministerial training. Mary had advertised in *Crusade* magazine (an outcome of Harringay) as a secretary looking for work. A complimentary copy of the same magazine reached Donald Ough working in Pall Mall in Acheson's, an oil firm. He needed a secretary and offered Mary the position. He was also responsible for relocating the firm's offices from Pall Mall.

Feeling uncertain, after three weeks I withdrew my notice and continued working at Covenanters and attending the Thursday lunchtime open-air services. Mary found herself, with new boss Donald Ough, relocated to Finsbury Square.

One Thursday the sound of my voice drifted upwards above the noise of the traffic. Mary looked out of the sixth-floor window of Acheson's office and said to herself, 'That's George somebody or other from the London Team.'

She, with her boss Donald Ough (a Christian believer), supported the open-air ministry. Handing out tracts (leaflets with a Christian message), joining in the Friday lunchtime prayer meeting in Wesley's Chapel in Old Street. It was good to meet up again.

About this time a Christmas carol

Our first date, 16th December 1958

concert was scheduled for 16th December 1958 at the Royal Albert Hall. Two tickets were purchased and on Thursday 10th December, at the end of the open-air meeting, I tentatively approached Mary by the fountain and asked if she would like to hear the *Messiah* at the Royal Albert Hall. She answered in the affirmative.

Tuesday 16th December we dined at Lyon's Corner House Salad Bowl in Trafalgar Square and reminisced about Huntingdon and Primrose Lane near to where Mary lived. We sat in the upper tier seats in the Royal Albert Hall and sang 'Figgy Pudding'. Our friendship developed, we enjoyed being together, serving God in various ways. On one occasion on a Sunday afternoon making sandwiches for the London Embankment Mission to hand out to those sleeping rough under railway bridges, I met John O'Brien, same name but no relation. We had a good chat about being a Christian and arranged to meet but he didn't turn up; a letter said he *'had been lifted'* and was back in prison!

Sixty-one years later we still reminisce about our first date.

'I'm Glad You Said "Yes"' Makes Us Smile in Warm Appreciation*

During this time I was living in Reigate, Surrey at 71, Chart Lane. Ma and Pop Bailey, a retired couple from Bath, were housekeepers for Skipper Pinchback, a retired Army captain who worked for the Covenanter Union. Skipper had been granted a sabbatical. In his absence I was asked to oversee

....

* Michelle Obama ' A senior partner asks if you will mentor an incoming summer associate, the answer is easy: of course you will. You have yet to understand the altering force of a simple yes' P.92 Becoming Penguin Random House UK 2018 the work at a newly acquired training centre. My walk on the breakwater was about to become more focused.

Living in Reigate I was able to worship at local churches – the local Brethren Hall and St Mary's Church, where Michael Baughen was curate, destined to become rector of All Souls Church, Langham Place near the BBC and then Bishop of Chester. Holy Trinity, Redhill had a Covenanter group run by Curate Rev. Bruce Evans, a South African who later became Bishop of Port Elizabeth. I worshipped at Holy Trinity from time to time.

One evening a green coloured leaflet published by the Church Pastoral Aid Society (CPAS) caught my attention: 'Wanted Men for the Ministry'. The leaflet listed several qualifications needed for an ordained minister. I had one: I was over twenty-three years of age! I had no money, no O-levels, neither confirmed nor a member of the Church of England, yet I sensed God saying, 'I want you ordained in the Church of England.'

To say this was startling is an understatement but it set me thinking. I wrote to Ken Walters, the CPAS local representative, saying that I was poor material, with no qualifications but what did he think? He wrote back very encouragingly. 'Many of us were poor material, but that is no hindrance if God is calling.' He emphasised the challenge of academic work involved; the need to be selected for training.

Becoming a Church of England clergyman still amazes me. As an evacuee in 1940 in a Methodist Sunday school class in Stratton, near Bude (where the breakwater is) I remember having a vision of a white-robed person serving God. The green leaflet set me thinking: I was twenty-six years old wondering where my future lay.

Following Ken's letter I joined St Mary's Church, West Kensington (the church I'd heard being destroyed by a flying bomb on 16th July 1944). David Thompson was the vicar 1953–62 and Mike Drury his curate (1958–62). I was welcomed and became a committed member, PCC minute secretary, lesson reader and youth club leader. Open-air services in the parish streets and hospital visiting and ward services became part of my life.

I was confirmed in Saint Paul's Cathedral on 12th December 1959 by the Bishop of London, studied for O-levels with the Rapid Results College.

Attending a selection conference in Derby Retreat House in July 1960 was a rich experience. The attendees consisted of twenty or so men (no women then) who spent three days in residence with the selectors. The Bishop of Bath and Wells was chairman; another clergyman and three lay people interviewed each candidate regarding various aspects of their call to the ministry, their educational standards, theological understanding, church affiliation and personality.

The retired military man who interviewed me knew of a certain Major General Wilson-Haffenden (the General had been Chairman of the Executive Committee of the Evangelical Alliance during the Billy Graham Mission at Harringay Arena in the spring of 1954). Wilson-Haffenden was a humble man who did household shopping in Fulham North End Road market. He acknowledged a group of us from Fulham YMCA preaching in the open air one Saturday morning. A somewhat plummy voice said, "Wilson-Haffenden – ah yes, very good man, knew him in India, very good Bridge player – met him recently at the Palace Garden Party." I can't recall any particular question he asked about my call to the ministry.

I can only surmise that when reporting back to the other

selectors he said, 'O'Brien, ah yes, very good man. I think he'll be all right.' So I thank God for Major General D.J. Wilson-Haffenden!

Interspersed between all the above is the relationship with Mary Holman. Together we joined in the open-air service in Finsbury Square. We had been to the Royal Albert Hall for a carol service. I was very aware of her but wondered if I was being sidetracked in my call to the ministry. One Saturday night I was on duty at the YMCA (having been restored to fellowship). Being concerned about Mary I knelt in prayer in the Maltbys' lounge and told God that I surrendered, I would not continue any deeper relationship. Then it was as if a wave sounded on the breakwater: 'Fear not to take . . .'

I found a Bible, opened it to Matthew 1:20 and read the angel's message to Joseph in his uncertainty. 'Fear not to take unto thee *Mary thy wife*.' It was a word from God not for Joseph but to George.

After Sunday-morning breakfast, a flurry of phone calls located the Holmans' telephone number in Huntingdon – Dora Holman gave 'George O'Brien of the London Team' Mary's phone number in Ilford. No lunch was eaten that day as I met Mary at Marble Arch. We found two deck chairs in Hyde Park and I made known my feelings, my background, inadequacy, and the lack of a bathroom in my family home. Mary's response was positive and charming – she remembers our first kiss on that April day! We went to All Souls Church and then the YMCA for supper and said goodnight at Notting Hill Gate Underground Station.

I wish I could say that all went well afterwards but it was not so. I had one of my crises of life, as they say. Following that Sunday afternoon, having made known my feelings to Mary, going to church 'showing her off' to the Maltbys, then going home, I began to doubt. I wrote to Mary suggesting we had a trial period of separation to confirm our future relationship.

The letters Mary kept and which I re-read fifty years later reveal my feelings of inadequacy and sadly the shame I felt about my working-class background, the inadequacy of my home, being ashamed of my parents, believing them and myself to be inferior. It was a real crisis of faith caused by the devil's accusations. David Griffiths (a long-time friend whom I married to Ida in the 1960s) on the second day of his honeymoon said that he walked around and around in a turmoil of emotions. 'What have I done, what have I done?' He overcame his feelings and lived happily with Ida for years, rearing three children.

Fortunately, through the down-to-earth spiritual common sense of our mutual friends Mike and Pauline Young, a loving letter telling me not to be so foolish and to read C.S. Lewis's *Screwtape Letters* helped me to get over that hump. And we were able to resume an ongoing relationship.

During this period we holidayed in Bude where our breakwater is located. Looking in Thornton's jewellers shop window we saw an opal cluster ring with no price tag on it. Enquiring the price, £9 was withdrawn from my meagre nine guineas Post Office Savings account, leaving nine shillings. The ring was purchased, delightedly admired on Efford Down with views of the breakwater. Eventually Mary's finger received the ring on 16th September 1960.

Alongside this I was hoping for a positive result from the selection conference I had attended in July.

The envelope containing the news of the selectors' decision duly arrived. I met the postman as I walked to Shepherd's Bush Tube Station. I read the welcome news of my selection for training travelling on the Central Line to Liverpool Street Station. Meeting Mary I handed over the envelope. We met for lunch and Mary had written on the envelope, 'Then were the disciples glad' (John 20:20), words we had both read in our daily Bible reading that morning which summed up our emotions exactly.

It seemed significant to me that Clifton Theological College, Bristol where I trained, came into being in 1932, my birth year! The Rev. David Thompson, vicar of St Mary's West Kensington, who arranged my confirmation at St Paul's Cathedral, gave me a book inscribed, 'His workmanship, created in Christ Jesus unto good works, which God has before ordained that we should walk in them' (Ephesians 2:10). He'd recommended Clifton Theological College as a good training college.

Meeting the principal, Tom Anscome, I was delighted to be offered a place for a three-year General Ordination Exam course. Clifton and other Evangelical colleges were riding high at that time through a resurgence of many men (blessed through the ministry of evangelist Billy Graham during the Harringay Arena Mission in 1954) applying for training for Church of England ministry. Because a Clifton student wanted a gap year for PhD study in Cambridge a place became available to me.

It is fortunate that Mary kept all the letters I wrote to her from Bristol. They give an authentic account of life in a theological college in the 1960s. I was required to have passed three extra O-levels of the five required qualifying for starting the General Ordination Exam course.

The Church of England finance board agreed to help fund my course, as did the Church Pastoral Aid Society. The book list was daunting for someone out of education for some years, especially New Testament Greek. But I was greatly anticipating going to college. A letter from the college Head Student was warmly welcoming.

Clothes and books were sent on ahead, packed in a tea chest. Mary saw me off from Paddington Station. She found the 'tongue in cheek' bereavement card I'd sent to her office in Finsbury Square, commiserating her loss! The train journey to Bristol, being met at the college by Berry Capron, settling in to student life is graphically recorded in eighty letters sent to Mary and saved in our Golden Wedding Anniversary Folder.

I delighted in being at theological college with godly, gospel believing, Bible teaching lecturers Peter Dawes, Michael Farrer and Alex Motyer. Clifton in the 1960s was an all-male college. It subsequently went through turmoil and change. Now, in the twenty-first century, amalgamated with Tyndale Hall and Dalton House, Trinity College Bristol has a high reputation. As one of the older men in college I delighted in the daily life, structure and order of college life.

However, before I'd sat any of the GOE exams, my breakwater place as a curate was determined. Peter Street, vicar of St James's Church, Carlisle required a curate in 1962 and interviewed men in Tyndale and Clifton Colleges. I knew of him. He knew of Mary's parents in Huntingdon and was familiar with Covenanters. I joined the group of men he interviewed at Clifton but explained that my course didn't finish until 1964. It transpired that he had two curates and would need a replacement in 1964. A weekend visit to Carlisle confirmed the rightness of the decision. So it was that God had planned that part of the breakwater walk. 'We won't tell the Bishop (Thomas Bloomer) yet; he'll have kittens.'

Seated next to Nick Carr (Director of Carr's Biscuits of Carlisle) that weekend I watched Carlisle United at home to

Queen's Park Rangers. Don't remember which team won. But I think QPR lost!

Marriage

I have never had a moment's doubt about marrying Mary – the tremendous blessing, help, support and loving care she has given to me and our family has made the ministry meaningful and enjoyable. Recently, whilst drafting these memoirs, a spontaneous compliment was given (May 2012). A couple were interviewed for the post of vicar of Doxey; Susan Corcoran (treasurer) said the new man's wife Rachel 'is just like your Mary: a "perfect vicar's wife"'. That doesn't mean that we've always seen eye to eye on every aspect of married life; 'Divorce,' said Ruth Graham about Billy Graham, 'never – murder yes, never divorce.'

Engaged 16th September 1960

We married at St Mary's Church, Huntingdon, on Saturday 14th July 1962. It rained. Mary, in a borrowed wedding dress of Gwen Forbat's, her bridesmaids were Susan O'Brien and Annabelle Spooner. The camera, promising

*St Mary's, Huntingdon
14th July 1962*

a pictorial record of the occasion, had a dud film. Andrew Forbat was best man. My Father disdained formal dress and wore a lounge suit – top hat and tails was too much for him, I love him for it! The key to a case full of belongings was left behind which meant a bus trip back to Huntingdon for me. We stood out like a sore thumb on the crowded commuter train into London from Cambridge. One regret we have is that we should have gone to a smart Cambridge hotel for our wedding night instead of the three-star B&B. We honeymooned in Cornwall at another modest accommodation. It rained again! The beach was full of pebbles, and we were not mobile. After three days we told the proprietor we were leaving. A bus took us to Stratton. Mrs Cobbledick wasn't taking in lodgers any more but her daughter Ivy was, and so developed another friendship – with Ivy and Den Gardner – on our breakwater which lasted years. We had survived the 'I don't want to get into bed with you' cry on our wedding night to be greatly blessed with three children: Marina born on 1st January 1965; David born on 21st November 1966 and Jonathan born on 8th August 1969.

Married Life in Bristol and Carlisle

We moved from London to Bristol, transported in a hired van driven by Ron Penny, an-ex Covenanter who as a missionary has lived in India over fifty years. We lived at 45, Downs Cote Drive, renting accommodation from a retired missionary Bishop Percy Stevens. Mary obtained a secretarial post in Avonmouth – better pay than London rates! – having a lift each day to and from work with David Addison, a surveyor for the Port of Bristol Authority working at Avonmouth Docks. David and his family lived opposite us in Downs Cote Drive.

Joy ensued when Mary announced that she was pregnant with our first baby. Full term came, the waters broke and Mary went into hospital for the delivery. Joy turned to sadness at the stillbirth of our first son on 7th September 1963. Bishop Percy Stephens gave us a framed verse:

Disappointment, His appointment
Change one letter and you'll see
That the thwarting of Thy purpose
Is God's better plan for thee.

We seemed to cope with the sadness of loss. I arranged an interment (no hospital provision in 1963). Tom Anscombe, the college principal, officiated and our firstborn 'David' was committed 'earth to earth, ashes to ashes' in an unmarked grave in a Bristol cemetery. Mary was in hospital several days under observation; subsequent births were likewise carefully monitored.

Following the loss of our baby Mary resumed work. I continued studies. As one of the older men, out of formal education for some years, I delighted in the daily life, order and routine of college life – playing hockey, swimming in the college swimming pool (the old orangery), being part of the garden maintenance team. Pastoral work included visiting a retired Church Army Sister who sang,

Standing somewhere in the shadows, you'll find Jesus,
He's the only one who cares and understands,
Standing somewhere in the shadows you'll find Jesus,
And you'll know Him by the nail marks in His hands.

The challenge of applying one's mind to theological study was willingly accepted. To find that some marks were up amongst those of university graduates was a great encouragement. I finished my three-year course as an 11/12ths Graduate having gone down in New Testament Greek, the Bishop of Kensington agreeing to 'exempt' me from taking Greek again – not many people know that!

In August 1963 news of a spectacular robbery hit the headlines. The Great Train Robbery, as it became known, became part of my walk on the breakwater! Among the names of the fifteen men involved was James Hussey – 'Surely not Jim Hussey who was in Highwood Hospital, a member of the Swifts, my Scout Patrol in 1947?' But yes, it was the same person. He had become an expert pickpocket and in 1958 had been sentenced to three years for a warehouse break-in and grievous bodily harm. Our steps on the breakwater were to get closer.

Two years of married life in Bristol were enjoyed; wives were welcomed into college, sharing Sunday worship and occasional lectures with visiting speakers. Living opposite us in Downs Cote Drive were the lovely Addison family, David and Pat with their three children Katherine, Richard and Hilary.

During the vacations I earned some money decorating and becoming a part-time postman over the Christmas period.

And so Graduation Day arrived in June 1964. During the service in St Mary's Church those leaving were presented with the blue-edged college hood and given a Diploma of Graduation.

Thomas Bloomer, Bishop of Carlisle Diocese, wanted

to see George O'Brien before ordaining him. A meeting was arranged in Christ Church opposite Euston Station in London. Our meeting was animated as we discussed some theological point. It became memorable when a cleaning lady soundly told us to be quiet. The bishop pulled his coat collar up, so she never knew that she had reprimanded a bishop of the Church of England!

The Archdeacon of Carlisle was most helpful giving advice and arranging that the Evangelicals to be ordained could be robed in cassock, surplice, scarf and hood and not a stole, the General Synod pronouncing that this was permissible. A pre-ordination exam paper was written, being adjudicated by Billy Jackman of St Mary's West Kensington in his sitting room.

....

[6] B Mansell Ramsay (1849–1923)
[7] Dawn Robinson Walsh, *Bude Through Time* (Amberley Publishing 2013) p.13
[8] Frank Colquhoun *The Harringay Story* (Hodder & Stoughton 1955) p.86

CHAPTER 5

1964 –1968
Carlisle – Stafford

"I came into town," wrote John Wesley,
"and offered them Christ." [9]

. . . .

So we moved to Carlisle. Memory is vague about how and when we moved our goods and chattels from London. Indeed, when we first heard of Carlisle we had to look on the map to see that it was located at the west end of Hadrian's Wall, in the north-west of England in Cumbria. Emperor Hadrian started the wall defence fortification in AD 122. Sad to say we didn't get to walk it during our years in the city. Carlisle is a lovely friendly county town, boasting a castle, and a cathedral dating from the twelfth century. Textiles, metal products and biscuits (Carr's!) are its main industries. We moved in good time to decorate 118, Dalston Road, which was to be our home during our curacy. Interestingly it was the same house that David Thompson, vicar of St Mary's West Kensington had lived in during his curacy 1950–1953.

Meanwhile we were accommodated with Adelaide Soal, a Japan Evangelistic Band retired missionary. We were thrilled to worship in St James's, an Evangelical church of great repute with worthy incumbents like Hugh Gough (who was instrumental in forming the Inter-Varsity Fellowship (1920s) and became the Archbishop of Sydney), George Duncan (a well-known Keswick Convention speaker), Herbert Cragg and others. Roger Bolton, whose family had strong links with St James's, was a member of the Covenanter group attached to the church; he currently works for the BBC as a journalist reporter.

We had anticipated joining the staff for some two years. The monthly magazine kept us in touch. Now we were about to become part of St James's church life.

The Archdeacon Rev. Charlie Nurse, an old-fashioned, godly man of the old school, transported me to the pre-ordination silent retreat at Rydal Hall. En route we inspected the Diocesan Youth Centre at St John's in the Vale, and enjoyed a walk on the fells, he in frock coat and gaiters, I in lounge suit!

The retreat at Rydal Hall over two nights was not the most meaningful for a Conservative Evangelical. Not used to silent retreats, time was wasted in the library looking for 'light' reading and surreptitiously conversing with others.

The interview with the Archdeacon, a High Churchman who emphasised the privileges of 'Priestly' ministry, was lost upon me then. I have subsequently been able to appreciate what he was talking about.

Being ordained Deacon on 27th September 1964 was memorable. On Monday 28th there was a Diocesan Conference in Carlisle Cathedral, Tuesday 29th was my appointed 'day off'. Parish work started on Wednesday 30th, following up contacts made during the summer Scripture Union holiday mission. My first call was Number 10, Waldergrave Road, the Leslie family. Their twin boys had gone to the mission meetings. Frank Leslie came to the door and we conversed for some fifteen minutes, arguing the toss about the 'hypocrites who went to church and told you to move when you sat in their pews' and a challenge to go to

Left: Greystoke, Cumbria 27th September 1964

Below: 'Priesting' 26th September 1965

St James's and find that it wasn't like that. We arranged to meet again. It was then I discovered that Myra, his wife, on the day of my call had been inadvertently locked in the bathroom. Frank had left the kitchen door ajar, which fouled the bathroom door and hindered Myra's exit!

Frank and Myra had married on 3rd February 1953 at St Barnabas's Church; they were blessed with three sons: twins Neil and Stuart born on 4th February 1958, and Robin on 3rd May 1963. After several visits 'propping my bike against the wall under their living room window' and answering their questions, in November 1965 both Frank and Myra came to faith, trusting the Lord Jesus as their Saviour. It was a wonderful seal upon my call to the ministry that the first people I spoke to became Christians. Myra wrote in March 2019 that I gave Frank my wedding suit – I had forgotten! We've kept in touch. Frank died on 7th December 1989. Myra had been concerned that Neil had a drink problem since 1990. Reading about Jonah with UCB notes[10] she was challenged to let God deal with the situation (a 'big fish' swallowed Jonah). Neil was near to death with cirrhosis of the liver. During 2000 Myra had entered into the blessing of 'tongues', that special gift of a language from the Holy Spirit (1 Corinthians 12 – 14). We agreed to pray in tongues at twelve noon for forty days (a day for Neil's age). Myra wrote in July 2003, 'Not only did the Lord bring Neil back from the jaws of death but took away his appetite for alcohol completely. Praise God!' The consultant was so amazed at Neil's recovery that he swore! Neil lived for another ten years, dying 20th September 2013. Myra in 2019 is still rejoicing in God her Saviour. She listens in to TBN UK Christian TV channel and says, 'I'm unable to get to church so instead of one sermon a week I have at least two a day.' She is a blessing and full of the joy of the Lord.*

Jim Humphreys with his wife Ann had been in post one year and was senior curate when we arrived. We blended, Northerners from Liverpool with their 'grass' and the Southerners from south of Watford with their 'graas'. We were thought to be very laid back.

Parish visiting, the Covenanter group, many funerals – some two or three or more at a time as the City Crematorium was part of St James's Parish. As part of my training I attended a funeral service conducted by Peter Street. Nervously, at my first funeral, with a family unknown to me, I committed 'our brother' earth to earth, etc. then realised that the coffin contained a 'sister'!

Clergy Team St James', Carlisle. Back row: Peter Street, Jim Humphreys, me; Ladies: Catherine Street, Mary, Anne Humphreys, Joan Anders

....

* Myra died 12th June 2020

With Joan Anders as parish worker we became a committed team of four, enjoying each other's gifts and abilities. St James's had long held a reputation as an Evangelical church. Prayer Book services were held each Sunday with Holy Communion at 8am; Morning Prayer at 11am; Evening Prayer at 6.30pm. Easter Day Communions started at 7am followed by 8 and 9am services.

From September to December Mary was pregnant with our next baby; it seemed delightfully appropriate at the Christmas carol service as she read the lesson 'Mary, being great with child'.

The people welcomed us with opened arms and Christmas gifts. On New Year's Eve on leaving church I went 'First Footing', the custom of being the first foot in the door after midnight. It was very popular in Scotland and the north of England then. Unfortunately all was not well at home as Mary was having birth pangs and didn't appreciate her spouse being absent. Mrs Street took us to the maternity hospital where Marina Kate arrived – a New Year's baby born on 1st January 1965 and had pride of place on the front page of *The Cumberland Evening News*. Waiting in the corridor to see mother and child the cheery words from an Irish man, *'Good morning, Father'* greeted me. I smiled and said to myself, 'You don't know how right you are.' Easter 1965 Marina was inundated with some two dozen Easter eggs!

Marina's birth, 1965

One day Stan Armstrong, a retired C.I.D. Inspector who sang in the choir, visited to enquire about one 'James Hussey' who was serving thirty years as one of the Great Train Robbers. How did I know him? Was I in anyway involved? I had written to Jim and was obviously being 'sussed out' by the Home Office! After some time I visited Jim in Hull prison (he asked for a Chaplain's visit.) It was strange to meet up again after some twenty years. Another visit was arranged when he was transferred to Wormwood Scrubs.

My visits didn't appear to have much spiritual influence. I lost touch with him. He was released in 1975. Later he had a criminal conviction in Germany. In 1989 he was convicted of trafficking cocaine and sentenced to seven years. He eventually died in St Christopher's Hospice, Sydenham in November 2012. So ended one relationship during my walk on the breakwater.

Christmas 1966 saw the first of our annual letters. They are a revealing reminder of those days on the breakwater. November 21st 'the telephone rang at 6.15am to say that David had put in an 8lb 2oz appearance half-an-hour earlier, so making us a family of four'. The letter records that 'we are still thoroughly happy in Carlisle' after over two years. The vicar, Peter Street, had asked if we would be prepared to stay an extra year. We did and celebrated St James's centenary in 1967 when previous incumbents and curates returned, among them David Thompson, vicar of St Mary's West Kensington, my 'sending church'.

One of the geographical blessings is the magnificent scenery in Cumbria and Scotland. During our four years I climbed or 'walked up' on my own Ben Nevis (4,406ft) September 1966, with Covenanters scaled Scafell Pike (3,227ft) and Skiddaw (3,072ft). Snowdon (3,581ft) had to wait to be conquered until we moved south. But I lay claim to have been to the top of the highest mountains in Scotland, England and Wales.

Walking or cycling around the Parish changed when a Raleigh moped was bought. Riding was enjoyable until a dog aggravated by the high-pitched engine noise decided to retaliate. Unfortunately he limped away being hit by the front wheel. I hit the road and also limped away to Pat and George Doyle's house. They bandaged my knee and helped me back home.

In April 1967 the National Evangelical Anglican Congress took place at Keele University, the first of several conferences which would take place. Ten years later at Nottingham, Caister 1988 and Blackpool 2003. The rationale behind the congress was that Evangelicals had a poor image in the Church of England at large and needed 'to repent and change'. It was good to be part of a new movement and to be present at Keele with 1,000 other delegates, including thirty observers, Roman Catholic, Greek Orthodox and Free Church representatives. For me it was the first of many gatherings. I had become an 'Eclectic'[11] by invitation – men and women, under forty, of evangelical conviction. As a member of Diocesan Evangelical Fellowships, DEF's annual conferences at Swanwick Conference Centre became my 'retreat' for some thirty years. They were times of rich fellowship support, teaching, fun, enthusiasm and up-to-date developments both in new services, songs and hymn books. And even a new-fangled thing called a 'freezer' was on show.

I returned each time full of thanksgivings to God for men and women who loved Jesus and made known the gospel in many and varied ways.

When forty (the cut off age) arrived, many were apprehensive. 'What would we do?' Then some enterprising person had the vision of Senior Evangelical Anglican Clergy so was born SEAC which kept us in situ for another two decades until, in the course of time, both Eclectics and SEAC, having fulfilled their task, were disbanded. I was to become a member of Reform, a Conservative Evangelical organisation seeking reform according to gospel truths. Reform merged with Church Society in 2018 – 'Equipping God's People to Live God's Word' – a fellowship contending to reform and renew the Church of England in biblical faith.

The Sixties saw the growth of the Charismatic movement, stressing the ministry of the Holy Spirit; Michael Harper, curate of All Souls Church Langham Place being very influential. Other groups formed, Reform amongst them, out of concern for the way certain doctrinal issues were being recognised in the Church of England – women's ordination, homosexual awareness. Michael Harper leaving the Church of England was welcomed into the Orthodox Church. Born in 1931, he died on 6th January 2010.

Jim and Ann Humphreys left to take on another curacy. In August 1966 Walter and Ann Wade joined the team. Walter had been in the Navy before ordination; we blended well.

New Year 1968 saw Peter Street leave to become vicar of Cheadle Hulme. This gave me more responsibility, but also created some upset when insisting upon a firmer baptismal policy.

Disputes over infant baptism were to become a further difficulty later on in my ministry. However, having to make decisions and chair PCC meetings was good experience.

Eventually Peter Downham was appointed as vicar and we stayed on for some three months as he settled in. We also had moving plans; *The Church of England Newspaper* of 5th April 1968 announced that we were appointed to the Parish of St Thomas's and St Andrew's Stafford. It was to be a long walk on the breakwater there, with many events and experiences.

....

[9] James S Stewart *Heralds of God* (Kessinger Publishing 2010)

[10] The United Christian Broadcaster's *The UCB Word for Today Bible study notes* www.ucb.co.uk/word-for-today

[11] The Electic Society was founded in 1783 by John Newton, rector of St Mary Woolnoth. It was refounded in 1955 by John Stott, vicar of All Souls Langham Place

A WALK ALONG THE BREAKWATER

CHAPTER 6

Moving from Carlisle (1964–1968) to Stafford (1968–1988)

*When we walk with the Lord,
In the light of His Word,
What a glory He sheds on our way!
While we do His good will,
He abides with us still,
And with all who will trust and obey!*[12]

· · · · · · · ·

Trains en route from Euston Station London to Carlisle run through Stafford. Trains in the Sixties moved past Henry Venables Ltd wood yard in Doxey. Stacks of timber – oak, ash, elm – piled high alongside the railway track were very noticeable. Venables, a family run business, produced quality, prestigious work. In 1985 it was advertised that 'giant English oaks' were required for the replacement and repair of York Minister roof after a thunderbolt struck. (Some said the damage was an act of God in retaliation for David Jenkins, the Bishop of Durham, expressing doubts about the virgin birth and the resurrection.) Following the fire at Windsor Castle, too, Venables were involved with restoration work. The Venables family worshipped at the Christian Brethren Assembly in the centre of town, adjacent to St Mary's, the parish church where State and Crown Court services are held with judges in attendance.

We had little awareness of or thought of ever living on the Stafford part of the breakwater as we journeyed but we were destined to spend a long time there. Stafford lies between the six pottery towns of Hanley, Burslem, Fenton, Longton, Stoke-on-Trent and Tunstall, and the Black Country of the West Midlands. It didn't appeal to many but we were excited about our move.

Jim Duxbury(1933–2017), an ex-member of St James's and vicar of Tittensor, had declined the offer of St Thomas's Stafford. Knowing that I was available, he passed my name to the Hyndman trustees. They duly invited me to visit the parish 'with a view' as the Free Church has it. It was a significant occasion when we, with Marina and David, visited early in 1968.

Churchwardens Allan Wilson and Bert Hanham met with me in Station Hotel. St Thomas's in Castletown and St Andrew's in Doxey were visited. Subsequently a notice in *The Church of England Newspaper* on 5th April announced our appointment to the living. Wednesday 3rd July at 7.30pm was the date of my institution as vicar of St Thomas's Castletown. The first incumbent in 1866 was the Rev. William Kendall BA; he resigned in 1897. I was the tenth incumbent. Bishop Stretton Reeve said that Carlisle Diocese had commended me. The Archdeacon installed me; I rang the church bell appropriately. On Sunday 7th July I 'read myself in', reading all the Thirty-nine Articles declaring that I believed these statements of doctrine which the Church of England professed. This obligation was duly witnessed by A.E. Hanham, J. Walters and R.J. Lucas who signed the appropriate document. The Articles are found at the back of the Book of Common Prayer. Though in 2019 new incumbents affirm that the faith of the Church of England is in agreement with the Articles they are not required to read them on their first Sunday.

St Thomas's Church Castletown was of very straightforward style, not prestigious: the nave 78ft by 28ft; the chancel 28ft by 20ft. The church was built of stone; the dressings of Grinshill stone from near Shrewsbury and the walling from Lancashire. The church was completed in 1866 and consecrated on 6th May 1866.

It was to be a challenging walk along this part of the breakwater. It had seemed strange to be greeted by Johnny Lunt, a Doxey resident, with 'Hullo, Vicar' before I'd been inducted to the living. I'd been called 'Batman' by a cheeky lad in Carlisle when wearing a long black cape, but never 'Vicar'; but now I was one! Our Christmas letter of 1968 says 'we now feel very much at home' here.

But there were stresses and strains to come, particularly over the question of infant baptism. Not the efficacy of the sacrament, but the practice. Before ordination I had been challenged by Free Church believers who stressed that baptism is for believers, and babies are too young to understand and respond. This had been a problem to me until I read *Outlines of Christian Doctrine* by Bishop Handley Moule (1841–1920) and discovered Covenant theology. As Abraham in the Old Testament had circumcised his children before they understood the significance of the Covenant relationship, so children of believers are part of the Covenant family of God through the shed blood of Christ on the cross, and sacramentally are declared to be 'born again' though needing subsequently to have a personal faith acknowledged in Confirmation. My problem was (and still is) when unbelievers request baptism without any indication of their own faith. 'Why do you want your baby baptised?' received unsatisfactory answers or no answer at all; like the father who thrust service card and baptism booklet into me with a 'Can't be bothered with this.'

On Thursday 9th January 1969 *The Staffordshire Advertiser* front-paged a picture of me with 'Stafford Vicar in Row Over Baptisms'. It was a difficult time and I felt rather vulnerable walking around the parish thinking that residents were saying, 'There goes that vicar who's being awkward over baptism.'

It was, therefore, an encouragement to receive a letter from the Earl of Harrowby saying, 'I admire and respect your stand over baptism . . . nominal Christianity is fast becoming hardly worthwhile.' He also indicated that in his own sphere he had had to make a principled stand.

The situation rumbled on and in October 1972 it became headlines again, this time the Bishop of Lichfield calling me to give an account. The Church Council set up a working party to debate the situation; a service of Thanksgiving and Blessing was provided as part of instruction before any baptismal service. A letter was delivered to every house in the parish explaining the church's future policy. This was in line with many parishes across the country though not all bishops (including Lichfield) approved.

Over the years matters quietened down and I found that young children requested baptism and some mothers asked about confirmation. It led to many opportunities of speaking frankly about the Lord Jesus Christ to people who were not prepared to follow Him wholeheartedly.

Apart from the baptism debacle there was the thrilling situation of a new build. St Thomas's Church in Castletown near the Stafford railway station was not where many people lived and was due for closure and demolition. Doxey was developing; a new vicarage had been built five years before, adjacent to land designated for a new church.

It was an exciting time learning about building practice; meetings with architects, planning and designing a new church. I had been involved with St Mary's West Kensington, London, my sending church, which I heard destroyed by a 'flying bomb' in July 1944. I became a member and was on the PCC in 1959 when a new church was planned, then built, and finally consecrated in 1962.

Doxey new church was to be a centre of worship and activity for the whole of the parish. During the years of preparation the virgin site had a marquee erected for a missionary weekend service activity. A radio buff erected an aerial and sent his 'call sign' across the airwaves telling listeners where he was.

Piddling investment accounts in the local bank, earning 3-4 per cent interest, were lumped together, sent off to the Church Commissioners Investment Fund, where, with other monies, earned 8-10 per cent. Money was raised by selling two bells from St Thomas's and St Andrew's to the Whitechapel bell foundry in London, stained-glass windows to art deco shops in Chelsea and a set of Coronation coins went to auction in London.

I became unofficial 'Clerk of Works', constantly on site. It was both exciting and time consuming.

Rod Neal, a church member who worked for GEC, made an 8mm film. He spent many hours recording the demolition of St Thomas's Church in Castletown, the foundation-stone laying and building of the new church centre. The DVD showing this is an excellent and historic account. It was updated and reissued for the fortieth celebrations in 2015.

A unique feature is the baptismal font made from grinding wheels. The Universal Grinding Wheel Company's factory is within the parish boundary. The font, made by the factory workers, is a timely reminder of local industry, as indeed is all the Sanctuary furniture, made and donated by Venables timber merchants also located in the parish. One regret is that Stafford railway is not represented. The original St Thomas's was built as a 'railway man's church'; it would have been special to have had a cross made from some surplus train track!

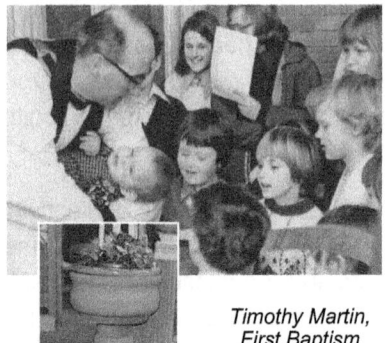

Timothy Martin, First Baptism in Unique Font, 16th March 1975

The total building cost plus furnishing and landscaping came to £66,000 with no debt outstanding. Today's prices (2019) would be in excess of £1.5 million. The church was dedicated on 8th March 1975.

Family

Looking back over the years spent along the Stafford, Doxey length of the breakwater, many events stand out. Jonathan, our second son, was born on 8th August 1969, bringing great joy to our family, keeping the nappy bucket plenished with soiled items. Terry cotton nappies needed regular washing, there being no disposable ones like today. Family life was full and enjoyable. Mary coped even without Dr Spock's advice; we seemed to fall into parenthood naturally.

We saw all three of our family grow into mature grown-up people. They all attended the local schools: Doxey Primary

Moving from Carlisle (1964–1968) to Stafford (1968–1988)

School, 'First School' in the old Stafford Grammar School, and King Edward High. All coped with the challenge of school, O-levels, A-levels and later on degrees and ONCs and HNCs.

As Mary didn't read Dr Spock I don't remember asking advice on how to be a father. Mary and I seemed to do what came naturally, though I do recall a nurse telling Mary to double up the feeding bottle dose to help Marina sleep contentedly. Now in our eighties, they in their fifties, we enjoy extremely good relationships with each of them. Fascinatingly different but equally loved and appreciated. Marina, New Year's Day baby, is artistic, able and alert. A qualified florist and PA graduated BA (Hons) from Oxford. Moody at times, keeping her cards close to her chest, she doesn't easily open up about personal matters, desires and aspirations. Thoughtful and helpful, my 'favourite daughter' who likes to 'walk on the breakwater' with me eating a doughnut!

David what can I say about him? Interestingly, the most spiritually alert at times, yet with his own 'cross' to bear. He publicly acknowledged his problems and was immersed in water, a renewal of his baptism. An excellent worker, diligent, correct, precise. We have spent many happy hours working together, me the DIY'er; he the professional. Me 'a blind man would be pleased to see it'; he applying himself to the task at hand. He is well qualified having 17th Regs up his sleeve, amongst other attainments. He has provided many Christian songs and hymns which he knows I appreciate, 'I Can Only Imagine' being particularly relevant. His greetings cards on our birthdays express his love thoughtfully. I thank the Lord for him whenever I view his work in the garage and look at the 'Godfathered' posts in the garden. He is proving his worth to his lovely wife Kathy, being fulfilled with more building enterprises in their home in Gloucester.

Jonathan and I share the same birthday month August: me 1932, he 1969. He is a whiz kid with IT; a graduate employed by Oracle, where he has worked diligently and consistently for over 20 years. He started a new job with Christians Against Poverty on Monday October 26th 2020. He is a prayerful man, though at times an anxious one. He opens up about personal needs more than his sister does. He's married to Bib (Isobel Wheat). I asked him the question: 'Will you take this woman to be your wife?' They are blessed with Isaac 19 and Amy 17. Jonathan can be rather sharp at times, but he's a wonderfully helpful person caring for his aged parents and married to a very capable and able lady. Sadly a year into their marriage Bib's mother died and we were back in church for her funeral; some years later her father also died. They are all equally loved and appreciated and we thank God for them.

On 16th March 1970, aged thirty-eight, I passed my driving test first go. A near neighbour, Bert Martin, ex-RAC and car mechanic, gave free driving lessons. To this day in a certain Stafford road I recall his advice: 'Go up to the grating ready to turn right'!

In 1983 we were overwhelmed with a gift of £500 'for a holiday'. Due to the miners' strike, accommodation on the Isles of Scilly was available for two weeks in August. The Isles have happy memories for us all. Marina especially would delight to spend a year on St Mary's experiencing the changing weather patterns. As a family we have enjoyed holidays in other locations. Mabledon House in Tunbridge Wells, Kent, is a large country mansion of some fifty rooms which Church Pastoral Aid Society (CPAS) used as a holiday conference centre resounded to gaiety, laughter and conversations from clergy families enjoying subsidised holidays. I also introduced the family to my evacuation location, Bude, from whence comes the title of these memoirs. One enjoyable day, late at night, as we neared our holiday accommodation, I said, "Shall we go for *a walk on the breakwater*?" Mary, conscious of the lateness of the hour and wanting to get the children to bed, demurred. Marina, David and Jonathan all exclaimed, "Oh yes, let's Dad." That late-night walk was bracing and enjoyable. Thus the expression, *'Shall we go for a walk on the breakwater?'* has become an aphorism for doing something different and exciting, and a title for these memoirs!

Life on a breakwater is not always easy; the waves can at times be overwhelming and the stones slippery. My walk along the breakwater was to be saddened. 'I've had a good day,' I said to Mary in 1969 a year after we had moved to Doxey. The phone rang; my brother had bad news about our mother. The gas meter in 47, Faroe Road was located in the passage outside the kitchen. It was quite usual for her to charge it. The penny coins fell 'clunk', 'clunk', 'clunk' into the meter collecting box. She went back into the kitchen, sat down by the gas stove, spread a towel onto a gas ring, gently laid her head down, covered herself with the towel and turned the gas on. Kate Ellen O'Brien, née Russell, my mother, born July 1902, took her own life by 'coal gas poisoning' in July 1969. My brother Charlie found her cold body some days later.

It was a sad ending. She had been a hardworking, loving mother, housekeeper – whitening the front door steps, toiling over steaming hot washing in the scullery on a Monday – and a caring homemaker. In her earlier days she had suffered from depression. During our teenage years she seemed to be under possibly menopausal stress; the three men in her life were not always understanding, loving and helpful. She used to read to me, I sitting alongside the chair she sat in. She came to my induction as vicar. She was a good, faithful, honest, hardworking woman. Will we one day meet again? Please God.

But further sadness came in June 1972 with the news that Mary's mother, Dora Holman, had died at home in a prayer meeting: one moment praying to the Lord, next moment in His presence.

Tragedy shook the church and, indeed, Stafford in 1985 with the dreadful news that three members of the Hawkins family, John, Monica and Michael their youngest son, had all been killed in an accident on the M1 motorway. It was a desperate time: the immediate family were devastated; the church family were overwhelmed. The Hawkins family had been associated with St Thomas's since 1928 when Monica's father had been vicar (1928–1939).

John was well known in GEC/EE as a researcher in the Nelson Laboratories. Approximately three hundred people attended their funeral on Thursday 17th January 1985. Simon Barrington-Ward, General Secretary of the Church Missionary Society, subsequently Bishop of Coventry (1985–1997), gave the address.

But there was also joy. Marina celebrated her twenty-first birthday on 1st January 1986. She also passed her driving test first time later that year.

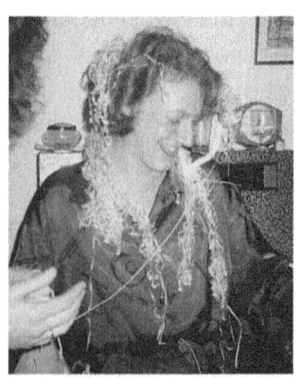

Marina's 21st 1986

Our Silver Wedding was celebrated with a secret pre-arranged event in the church on 14th July 1987.

Baptism in the Spirit

Our 1971 annual Christmas letter relates that in March I received the 'baptism in the Spirit' through the ministry

Our Silver Wedding 1987

of the Rev. Roy Jeremiah of the London Healing Mission in Notting Hill Gate. This 'baptism' resulted in the phenomenon of 'speaking in tongues'. Back in the fifties in YMCA days the Pentecostal church emphasis had been noted and rejected. I recall a friend speaking of it as 'shag a rag a bag dag' in dismissive tones. During the late1950s at home, kneeling by my bedside, I suddenly spoke out with strange words, and again the following day in Wesley's Chapel, but I didn't tell anyone. So it wasn't until March 1971 when the 'Charismatic movement' was well into being, led by the Rev. Michael Harper (1931–2010), that I met Roy Jeremiah of the London Healing Mission. It was a memorable meeting. 'Take off your glasses,' he said, 'and the thick walls are well built' – both comments bemusing to me until he started to minister. Laying hands on my head and commanding the 'unclean spirit' (more of this later) to depart. As I confessed my need, a cataract of tears flowed unceasingly from my eyes (so much more convenient without spectacles on!). I have never wept so much before or since. A perfect cleansing flow of relief and release. Then I bent forward in the chair, raised my clenched fist and roared out in a 'tongues language' rebuking the devil and bringing further relief.

That evening I travelled back in our Morris 1000 Traveller delighting in my release and new-found language. I became so intrigued that I recorded myself speaking in tongues and then playing the recording back to hear what it sounded like. Today (in 2019) as I write, the initial enthusiasm of the 60s and 70s seem to have mellowed. Alpha Courses and Messy Church emphasis dominate. Having been initially intrigued with the reality and veracity of 'tongues' I neglected the gift, until recently (2018), when it has become a regular part of my prayer life, a means of grace. 'He who speaks in tongues 'edifies' (*oikodome*) 'builds up' himself, says Paul in 1 Corinthians. Bishop Tom Wright says it 'shows that the King is in residence there'.

Over the years the ministry of the Holy Spirit was considered, discussed, taught and entered into. Not everyone was convinced; some left the church because we were too charismatic, others joined and stayed because of the emphasis. Michael Harper came and preached. Later he and his wife left the Church of England for the Orthodox Church, mainly through the ordination of women issue. One notable international woman Jackie Pullinger (author of *Chasing the Dragon*) came from Hong Kong and stayed with us, ministering both in Doxey Church and in Church Lane Evangelical Church. A number of people asked for ministry to receive the Holy Spirit in His fullness.

Jackie Pullinger from Hong Kong

Moving from Carlisle (1964–1968) to Stafford (1968–1988)

Ecumenically, working with other denominational persuasions was par for the course for me. Trevor Partington arrived as pastor of Covenant Hall, a Pentecostal church in Stafford. David Taylor became pastor of Rising Brook Baptist Church. Though of different denominations our common Evangelical faith united us and we became a recognised threesome whom God used to bring together Stafford churches in trust and cooperation, over several decades. Trevor Partington recalls his involvement with:

Telephone Ministry called 'God's Message'

This was a national organisation started by Norah Coggan, the sister of the then Archbishop of Canterbury. To have her preach at my church one Sunday morning when I had moved to Hereford was a strong reminder of the very real unity we have in Christ.' Trevor's role in the telephone ministry in Stafford was to collate the two-minute messages. I would record the messages onto tape with the help of Harold Bee, a church member, ready for transmitting over the telephone line. Three or four ministers were on a 'call back' facility. One caller asked, 'Is that God speaking?' 'No, but I can tell you how to get in touch'. Cliff Richard recorded two messages which received hundreds of calls. Diocesan Bishop Stretton Reeve, who didn't approve of my baptism policy, did like the telephone ministry and donated £25.

United Memorial Service

These services at the crematorium began on a trial basis in the early 1970s. The first service was held on 17th December 1972. Held four to five times a year to which between 100 and 150 mourners come. Facilities provided by the Borough

Council, services arranged by the ministers fraternal. Trevor is still co-ordinating them; the next scheduled date is 28th July 2019.

Joint Missions

We did several of these. It all started in the 70s with the Christian musical celebration *Come Together*. Rehearsals were held in the local Christian Brethren Hall (one Church of England couple, having lived in Stafford for fifty years, had never been in that church building). The musical was held in St Mary's Church which was packed to the gunnels each night. Following *Come Together*, in 1974 the local Council of Churches initiated a number of events. 1981 saw David Watson from York come with a team for a five-day mission. In 1986 the Catholic monk Ian Pettit with the Anglican Archdeacon John Delight shared the platform for a ten-day celebration proclaiming the gospel at central and area events.

More than twenty-five churches including all the main denominations met in November 1991 to plan for a mission in 1993, inviting 150 members of St Aldate's Church Oxford to share in a two-week evangelistic mission in September 1993. It happened.

There are so many memories of our Stafford breakwater walk. Lovely, faithful church members: Allan and Mary Wilson, John and Monica Hawkins and their family David, Ruth, Ann and Michael (the M1 tragedy is still raw), John and Susan Cocoran, Doreen Bennet, an able long-serving PCC secretary. They were there with others when we first arrived. Information about the church recorded that there were three lay readers attached to St Thomas's and St Andrew's. By the time we moved from Carlisle two had left, leaving Gordon

Bevans, a faithful man who preached simple and straightforward sermons. His favourite text was 'The unsearchable riches of Christ'. In the Lord's goodness, John and Ruth Clark joined the church fellowship and John became a valued reader. We did not always see eye to eye on some matters but we worked together in the ministry for a number of years. John also served on the General Synod for some forty years.

Our time in Doxey was blessed in seeing a number of men ordained: Stephen Beach, Daniel Corcoran, David Hawkins (Consecrated Bishop) and Stephen Wilson. Jane Wilson also went out as a missionary with the South American Missionary Society. After the new church was opened I kept a list of newcomers: from 27th July 1975 to 23rd October 1988 over two hundred visitors came, many remained as church members and faithful workers.

Third January 1982 records that Julie Perkin, ex St Mary's Stafford, converted at Bath University, turned up and stayed for the after-church fellowship meeting in the vicarage. Julie, married to Stewart Jones, has been CEO of the Lichfield diocese for over ten years., Returning home from her marriage 28th March 1992 we found we'd had burglars in! (See addendum.)

January 1986 saw Chris and Cath Powell and their children David and Rachael. They became firm friends. Chris worked on the *Stafford Newsletter* subsequently moving away and forming publishing firm Verité CM Ltd. Chris and Cath came to faith. Attending the Donnington Bible Convention; they opened their picnic hamper displaying bottles of wine, much to our then sensitive scruples! God will remember all those named or unnamed for their work of love and gift of faith.

During the twenty years as Vicar of the Parish I had experience of chaplaincy work in two establishments. The first was Stafford Prison, currently housing several hundred sex offenders (aged between young adults to a number of men in their eighties and nineties). The prisoners in 1977 were guilty of varied misdemeanours, with few sex offenders on 'Rule 22' secluded for their own protection. I was 'Substitute Chaplain' one day a week and covering extra services as appropriate. It was a good learning curve, my London 'working class' background helped me adapt, meeting men and youths with varied experiences. For two or three years I helped out. One particular prisoner, a Christian on day release, assisted with a school assembly at Walton High School. He made a stir when he told the assembled students that he was an inmate! Many volunteers regularly gave of their time and talents, notably the church organist, Marjorie Boothby, who played for many years in the Sunday services, also at Stafford Hospital. She was awarded an OBE.

The other chaplaincy work was at St George's Hospital, the psychiatric institution, the old asylum. The resident chaplain had four hospitals in his remit and asked the chapter of local clergy if anyone was available to assist one day a week. Having given up the prison chaplaincy I felt obliged to offer my services. It was whilst being on-call during this period that these memoirs obtained part of their title. It was late in the night during 1987 the hospital phoned wanting the on-call chaplain. 'Have you called the Catholic chaplain?' I enquired and heard the telephonist ask a colleague, *'Have we called the Catholic chaplain? I've got the ordinary one on the phone'!* Thus part of the lovely anecdotal title for these memoirs came into being.

CHAPTER 7

Chaplaincy 1988–1999

'I pray that you may be active in sharing your faith,
. . . some benefit from you in the Lord;
refresh my heart in Christ.'
(Philemon vv. 6,20)

. . . .

A letter dated 9th June 1988 sent to all PCC members informed them of my acceptance as full-time chaplain at St George's and Kingsmead Hospitals in Stafford. It brought tears to one member who received it! I had been doing some part-time chaplaincy work at St George's for some months. It was worthwhile ministry where I was free to visit any department, wards and occupation therapy units. The substance abuse unit welcomed my input and from time to time I invited a client to Sunday lunch. Charles Handy, author, relates when a school wanted students to set a table which way the knife and fork should be laid: 20 per cent said one way, 40 per cent said another, but 40 per cent didn't know because they had never sat at a table with others for a meal.

We, too, found that one young woman said, 'I've never done this before' when we sat down to eat a meal. Another client received a total surprise of £100 which a Christian visitor said God prompted him to give as a gift.

One Friday afternoon as I left the site a voice called out, 'Goodbye, George.' One of the patients was acknowledging me. I felt humbled to be so recognised. Because hospital chaplaincy was suiting me I applied and was short-listed for a Leicester hospital job. After two interviews I was offered a post. For various reasons it didn't seem right so I declined and applied for the Stafford post, which had been advertised but no appointment made. So it was that when the chaplaincy was re-advertised I eventually applied. It was exciting to be interviewed; my interest in making garden compost drew questions from one panel member. I was offered and accepted this next fulfilling walk on the breakwater. There were to be new vistas and people to meet as I travelled along. I was licensed as full-time chaplain at St George's and Kingsmead (a geriatric hospital), both on site, on 1st November 1988 by the Bishop of Stafford the Rt Revd Michael Scott-Joynt (1943–2014). Michael Scott-Joynt had become the Bishop of Stafford in 1987. A tall man (6ft 7ins) with a gracious nature, he and his wife Lou became our good friends. He was appointed Bishop of Winchester 1995–2011. He took a traditionalist stance on same-sex relationships and condemned the 'cruel evil' of 9/11. His death in 2014, aged seventy-one, from cancer was a sad loss. We remember him with affection; I wear the cross he dedicated with a thankful heart. At my licensing Archdeacon John Delight preached the sermon with a visual aid block of wood, which initially appeared obscure but illustrated the name 'Jesus'. The chaplain's task, he said, was to reveal Jesus in one's life and ministry.

Leaving the vicarage in Doxey meant finding a new house to live in. When most couples of our age, in their mid-fifties, were completing their mortgages, we were about to start one.

Our house at 185, Tixall Road is a 'Scrase built' house of the 1930s. Scrase was a well-known Stafford builder. The house is a solid brick-built construction of excellent workmanship. Double 'purlins' span a large 15ft-by-15ft loft area (eventually being fashioned into an art-studio-cum-den). Meeting our next door neighbours we were informed that we would be residing next door to savages! John and Sue Savage in fact. They even gave us carte blanche to use their home for extra accommodation whilst they were on holiday. We continue to enjoy a warm and friendly relationship. Sue is a great help playing the piano when I celebrate Communion at St John's Church.

We were able to reside in the Doxey vicarage for some eight months (rent free as caretakers) whilst we added an extension. Clive Spencer drew up plans for an extended kitchen, utility room and extra bedroom; Jim Fellows laid the bricks, David and Jonathan laboured with me mixing compo, digging trenches, laying new water supply pipes, and taking down a small chimney. Between us we transformed a solid building into an excellent piece of real estate. Scaffolding was provided free of change by a 'churchwarden' sales rep from the hospital. We were conscious of God's gracious provision. During this activity another of our title anecdotes happened. An RSJ (rolled steel joist) was needed to support part of the new extension; I visited the local scrap yard replete with my dog collar. As is my wont I enquired of the scrap merchant if he was religious and believed in God. I answered his negative reply with, 'Oh, He's quite a friend of mine.' Returning next day to pay my debt the RSJ was marked not with my name but 'God's Mate'. The so inscribed RSJ now firmly supports our fourth bedroom!

RSJ with inscription

Chaplaincy work suited me. From teenage years, in hospital with pleurisy, I had an unfulfilled interest in nursing, so I fitted in well to the routine of hospital life, being 'on-call' during the night hours, dealing with traumatic situations, accidents and emergences, bereavements. Able to pray with and support relatives was a special privilege. Letters of appreciation confirm the blessing it was to some people. Not everyone was receptive; having waited half an hour for a young woman to arrive at the bedside of her dead relative, her response to my 'Let us pray' was 'I don't want to bloody well pray' and stormed out of the room. Another particular unexpected comment in the middle of the night from waiting relatives was, 'You had our High Cross baby pram for your son Jonathan,' which set me back somewhat. It transpired that the lady in question had advertised her unwanted pram in the *Stafford Newsletter*. Mary going to view it discovered that both babies using the pram were named Jonathan. The lady seeing my name badge remembered us and made the remark. It certainly eased the situation of her mother's illness.

Being Chairman of the Ethics Committee was a responsibility which had not been mentioned in the job description. It was a challenge chairing a committee of high-powered able doctors, consultants and professional lay people. The regular discussions concerning ethical implications with some procedures or trials were enthralling. I felt my responsibility (apart from controlling the meeting) was to 'ask the dumb question' which often enlightened matters. During my tenure it was good to attend countrywide training courses with eminent speakers opening up on ethical issues.

The New King James Version Bible presented at my institution by Ken Rider, the hospital administrator, was inscribed with words from Philemon encouraging me to 'refresh' the hearts of patients, relatives and staff. The frontispiece lists details of some fourteen people from April 1989 to April 1999 whose lives had been changed, though contact with some has been lost. It is a lovely reminder of a varied ministry. It was a great joy and blessing to have had the opportunity of hospital Chaplaincy.

The appointment involved being available to staff as well as patients. Two consultants came at different times to ask for prayer, indicating that we are all 'from the dust and to the dust we shall return' fragile creatures who need to relate to our Maker and Redeemer.

An IRA attack on Sir Peter Terry, a Deputy Supreme Allied Commander in Europe who lived in retirement near Cannock Chase, happened in 1988. He was seriously injured. It was a privilege to take Holy Communion to him and his wife on Easter Day. The Bible reading was about Peter the disciple going to the tomb. Sir Peter was unable to open his mouth so I intictured the wafer, touched his lips with the consecrated elements which his wife consumed. Sir Peter made a recovery and was present at the consecration of the hospital chapel some years later, which Terry Waite 'opened'.

During these years I maintained contact with the Stafford Council of Churches being chairman of the General Committee and of the local Bible Society committee. In 1990 we worshipped at Castle Church; Terry Pye with his wife Gay came to take on the incumbency. They had three children Elizabeth, Stephen and Timothy. They had been missionaries with OMF (Overseas Missionary Fellowship) in South Korea. We became close friends, enjoying their company and sharing several holidays to St David's in North

Wales and a notable holiday to the United States in October 1992 where we got damp from the spray of Niagara Falls, flew over the Grand Canyon, saw where Buffalo Bill was buried; ate waffles, pancakes, steak and put on too much weight! I met Margaret Coleman, last seen thirty-eight years before in the Billy Graham office in Gate Street, London during the Harringay Arena Mission. We also stayed a week with Andrew and Gwen Forbat in Swannanoa in the Smoky Mountains, North Carolina.

Hospital Radio Stafford was a regular feature when guests were invited to choose favourite music they'd like to hear whilst in hospital. George Mellor interviewed me in 1993. My interests included Don Francisco, The Bricklayer, Brown Boots and 'When the Roll is Called Up Yonder I'll Be There'. A hundred copies of the DVD will be available when these memoirs are printed.

September 1993 saw 'Awakening '93' when 100-plus students, members of St Aldate's Church Oxford came for a week's mission, telling the story of God's love. Using many ways of communication – juggling, singing, drama, videos, loud music! – over a thousand Christians gathered for the final celebration service.

In St George's Hospital the chaplaincy department removed to a new smaller chapel located in St Chad's House, the former Kingsmead Hospital. The Roman Catholic Archbishop of Birmingham Maurice Couve de Murville performed the ceremony with Bishop Michael Scott-Joynt assisting. Fascinatingly, the chapel is built adjacent to the mortuary thereby illustrating that Jesus is the resurrection and the life to all who believe.

Mary and I celebrated our thirty-fourth wedding anniversary in 1996 with a surprise journey arranged by me via Milton

Keynes (Chris and Cath Powell), Witney (Pat and Ben), Wiveliscombe (Daphne Kelly), Barnstaple (Eldey Lloyd), and finally Bude where we had honeymooned. At St Olaf's Church Poughill, Leslie Keenan blessed us at the communion rail.

My sixty-fifth birthday was celebrated with a surprise luncheon party when seven of my ten godchildren were present. Mary planned it, making contact with somewhat out-of-touch godchildren; remarkably most of them made the occasion. Currently they are prayed for daily.

65th birthday party, my seven God-children surrounding me: back row, left to right,: Emily, Priscilla, Ruth, Bertie; front row, left to right: George, Matthew, Tom.

Other God-children are David Forbat, Andrew Neal and Joanne Leaver.

We celebrated our special birthdays in June 1998 with a Master Sun Holiday to Kaltern in Northern Italy, making new friends and planned another holiday to Malta in March 1999.

In 1994 my medical records show that I had a TIA (transient ischemic attack), a mild stroke. I recall sitting up in bed after a busy and rather frantic weekend of DIY sensing a pulse in my head with a weakness on my left side affecting holding a cup of tea. Various visits to a neurologist followed. Subsequently I was diagnosed with myasthenia gravis, which affects the immune system with muscle fatigue. This is now controlled with medication.

However, in July 1999 I retired. I had been on the payroll of the NHS since 1st July 1985 (part time) then full time from

1988 to 1999. It was a new learning curve being retired. I look back on the years in chaplaincy work with great satisfaction and thank the Lord for such worthwhile, fulfilling ministry.

CHAPTER 8

1999 Onwards: Retirement Years

'My walk with Jesus is much more important than my walking on the moon.'
(Charles Duke, Astronaut)

. . . .

This walk and activity along the retirement length of the breakwater includes evangelism, trusteeship of the Fulham YMCA and Permission to Officiate in the Diocese of Lichfield.

Evangelism

The word comes from the Greek New testament word *euangelion*, good news. A definition of evangelism according to the Lausanne Covenant (1974) 'To evangelise is to spread the good news that Jesus Christ died for our sins and was raised from the dead according to the Scriptures, and that as the reigning Lord he now offers the forgiveness of sins and the liberating gift of the Spirit to all who repent and believe.'

For me one of the fascinating aspects of eternity will be meeting people to whom I've witnessed. From the earliest days of my conversion I've wanted to talk about Jesus. Andrew Forbat, who led me to Christ, set a good example sharing his faith with others.

My son David set me thinking, 'What happened to people you've spoken to over the years. I know you like evangelising. Do you know what results there have been?'

A similar question was asked of an enthusiastic 'fisher of men', had he caught any fish? The reply, 'No, but I've influenced a few.'

That might be said of my own ministry. But it was at a gathering at Orators Corner, Marble Arch in 1953 that I cut my teeth in witnessing and unwittingly had my first convert.

Marble Arch in London is famous for the different groups which gather there on a Saturday evening: poets, political people, religious groups, anyone is free to get a soap box and spout the odds about this and that. Open-air evangelism, standing on a platform proclaiming about Jesus Christ keeps one alert.

I was with a group of the London Team (mentioned earlier) proclaiming the gospel of Jesus Christ. I was asked to speak to an ex-sailor who had seen the world who said, 'I've been a bad boy.' As I prayed with him he copied my words, so I made the prayer one of confession asking for forgiveness. He gave me his address and I gave him a New Testament. He lived near Victoria Railway Station. Stanley Seymour, a trainee London City Missioner, knew the address. 'Oh, not there – she's a real tarter,' speaking of the lady in the flat. He visited enquiring about the sailor and was confronted by an irate woman. 'Oh, so you're the reason – I don't know what's happened to him, he's changed.' One day perhaps in eternity I shall know what happened.

George Dempster, author of *Finding Men for Christ* and *Touched by a Loving Hand*, records remarkable accounts of men and women met, helped and transformed through his witness. In 1950 I discovered his books on a weekend camp at Whitsable with the Fulham YM Covenanter group, became gripped by the stories he recounted and wanted to emulate him, though not to have my teeth put out, as he did, by being slashed across his mouth by a brass scales dish wielded by an irate costermonger! I didn't always get it right; with the enthusiasm of youth I remember one night stopping a near neighbour in Faroe Road where I lived saying, 'I'd like to tell you what Jesus means to me.' He didn't want to know and continued on to his house a few doors away – that was over sixty years ago.

From the earliest days of my conversion up to writing these memoirs, sharing with others about Christ has been part of my life. I wrote a letter to a REME soldier in my brother's billet in 1950 which was duly delivered. My brother had said, 'There's a bloke like you back at camp,' so I wrote to share my faith but got no response. My brother, on the other hand, was always ready to argue about religious matters saying (after I was ordained) that if there was a God he would say, 'My brother's a vicar in Stafford,' and expect the good Lord to accept him on those grounds! Read on to discover what actually happened some years later.

Outdoor evangelism has always appealed; it was where Jesus spoke. Various places have resounded to my voice, especially of course Finsbury Square in 1958, but also Orator's Corner in London, the streets of St Mary's Parish West Kensington, the Downs at the top of Black Boy Hill, Bristol, St Ives market in Huntingdonshire, the main street of St Mary's, Isles of Scilly. Fulham's North End Road market on Saturday mornings saw a team from the Fulham YMCA witnessing to stallholders and their customers about Jesus, the Saviour of the world. Not everyone appreciated the message.

'You ought to go and clean someone's kitchen instead of shouting there,' said an elderly lady out shopping.

'Tell me where your kitchen is and I'll come.' (I was sincere.)

Rather prissily she said, 'My kitchen doesn't need cleaning,' and passed on.

My brother, unbeknown to me, one day stood in a doorway to listen to me preaching. He was surprised when I shouted out to all and sundry, 'And it's no good hiding away in doorways, God knows all about you.' I was told this story by his daughter Sue after he had died in 2003. The following is an account of what happened in 2003.

Memories of a Few Precious Days in Wales, March 2003

Monday, 17th March

'George.' It was a faint call I heard standing outside Carmarthen Railway Station. Mary and I had come to spend a few days with Charlie, his wife Eileen and daughter Sue. 'He's over there,' I said and we walked across to the car park. It was the start of four memorable days spent at Laugharne Park in South Wales.

The usually strong voice had been taken over by a hoarse, dry one and the familiar gait had become a slow shuffle due to his oedema. *'I'm pleased you're here. It's good to see you,'* he said. We talked a little as we made our way to chalet number 48. I remember remarking that it was next to 47 (47 being the old home number in Faroe Road, London).

Tuesday, 18th March – 'a' 'the' 'my'

Charlie was sitting propped up in bed. It was a pleasant day with the sun streaming through the bedroom window. What prompted me to go into his room at that moment I don't know – but I did want to be with him.

I sat on the bed facing him. He held my hand. He obviously wanted to talk.

'Does it seem selfish, now?' he asked. I told him about the 'a' 'the' 'my' thoughts I'd had the night before as I'd prayed for him. To many Jesus is 'a' Saviour – one amongst many. To others Jesus is 'the' Saviour – the only one. But it's really meaningful when you're able to say Jesus is 'my' Saviour!

Upper Street, Islington – Oxford Market and Jellied Eels

In 1997 Charlie and I had explored our roots visiting Ivinghoe Road, Dagenham where I'd been born (and where he'd tried to bury me in the back garden!). We also visited many of his old haunts – mainly pubs he knew around the Angel, Islington, and we went to 'Clarkes' in Oxford Market, near Upper Street, to eat pie and eels (Charlie loved jellied eels). But Upper Street, Islington was memorable to me for another reason – it was there on 4th July 1949 that I had asked Jesus to become 'my' Saviour.

'Doesn't it seem selfish?' he'd said.

'No, Jesus loves you and wants you to know Him. Anyway, Jesus told the story of the workers called at different times of the day. The last was paid the same as the first. Remember the hymn we learnt in Stratton (as evacuee boys)?

> *"'He called me, long before I heard*
> *Before my doubting heart was stirred*
> *But when I took Him at His word*
> *Forgiven, He lifted me."*

'All you have to do is say, "Jesus, I need you. Come into my heart."'

Without a moment's hesitation Charlie cried out, *'Jesus, I need you. Come into my heart.'* We hugged each other. Sometime later he told Eileen and Sue, *'I've got George's Jesus – eternal life.'* We were sitting in the lounge; I was surprised at this and said, 'I never said anything about witnessing, mate!'

That day we went to Saundersfoot, near Tenby, where we had cod and chips in Marina's Parlour.

Wednesday, 19th March

A very special day spent at the Botanic Gardens outside Carmarthen. Perfect spring weather – warm and calming. He sat in, and I pushed, the wheelchair. The Gardens are well worth visiting. The water feature of meandering rivulets, calm pools and pleasant tumbling falls, make a delightful scene. The ladies followed on at a slower pace.

We stopped and looked. What prompted us to sing together?

From sinking sands He lifted me
With tender hands He lifted me
From shades of night to plains of light
Oh, praise His Name, He lifted me

Charlie enjoyed two cups of coffee and ate some scrambled egg. *'That ham smells nice,'* he said.

Later, on the walk back to the car, he spoke of fine spring days and how he liked being in the garden and getting the beginning of a tan.

We stopped at the waterfall feature; he stretched out his hand and splashed the cool water over his head and face. I've thought about this since – was it a baptism – I wish I'd had my wits about me; I would have baptised him as a symbol of his newfound faith

Thursday, 20th March

In the other room Charlie had had a disturbed night. I held his photo in my hands and prayed for him in that Spirit-given 'language of tongues'. Eileen and Sue told us what happened.

He'd had some melon. They sat with him. He was staring. He's going. They held his hands. 'He's gone.'

At the Gardens the day before, waiting for the ladies, we'd talked of coming closer together over recent years. Then he murmured, *'My Saviour . . . I suppose after all I must have done something right.'*

I didn't say anything – only thought, 'Yes, Charlie, you asked Him in – that's what you did.'

I'm glad I looked up Psalm 18:4–6 (NIV), it was so appropriate:

> *The cords of death entangled me; the torrents of destruction overwhelmed me. The cords of the grave coiled around me; the snares of death confronted me. In my distress I called to the Lord; I cried to my God for help. From His temple He heard my voice; my cry came before Him, into His ears.*
>
> *Now on a higher plain I dwell*
> *And with my soul, I know 'tis well*
> *Yet how, or why, I cannot tell*
> *He should have lifted me."*

Some ten years later I wrote a fantasy about Charlie's thoughts. It is appended at the back of this book with other items of interest.

'Charlie'
Kenneth Charles O'Brien
Born: 20th January 1931
Died: 20th March 2003
Entered into 'Life':
Tuesday 18th March 2003

There are many opportunities for witnessing: one-to-one, handing out tracts (printed leaflets) or talking to people. As part of a keep-fit routine I went swimming at Stafford's recreational centre. The early morning walk along the river was pleasant. 'Andy' walked the other way to work at Alsthom and we greeted each other. During 2006 I stopped. 'Hi, I'm George.' He replied, 'I'm Andy.' So started a relationship which continues still in 2019. Andy loves philosophy and is agnostic about Christianity. We give each other books, meeting for a coffee or meal. He's not yet convinced that Jesus is the Way, the Truth and the Life. Pray for him.

On Saturday 24th August 2010 travelling on the Underground train from Fulham Broadway to Paddington I was recounting to my daughter Marina about my memoirs and David's comment about people I'd spoken to over the years. The man sitting next to me – tall, sun-browned, tattooed, wearing khaki drill trousers – had moved over to allow Marina and me to sit together. What prompted me to think 'Say something to this guy sitting next to you'? After a moment's hesitation I turned to him and said, 'May I invade your space?' He acquiesced and I told him I was planning my memoirs, being a retired clergyman, and my son wanted to know what happened to people I'd spoken to over the years.

The man's name was Jack and I asked him if he was religious. He replied that he had been brought up Catholic but wasn't practising. I shared with him that Jesus loved him and said, 'So you see, Jack, you'll go in my memoirs as someone I've spoken to.'

'I have to get out here,' he said as the train pulled into another station. 'Good luck with your memoirs.'

'That's the second bit of good news I've had today,' I said to the Jewson's delivery man off loading materials at the Fulham YMCA shop.

'What's the first bit then?'

'Jesus loves me, this I know for the Bible tells me so,' I replied.

My brother, the electrician working with me on the shop, was intrigued by this conversation and subsequently related it to his golfing colleagues some days later, so my witness was expanded.

During 2010, on a visit to my dentist in Stafford, I enquired if I could ask him a personal question. Thanking him for his dentistry expertise to me and my family I asked him (he knowing I was a minister of religion) if he believed in the Lord Jesus Christ? He wasn't put off by the question but explained that his scientific background and training made him uncertain. He then confided that his mother had recently died and he had apologised to the officiating minister that he didn't believe. The minister responded that God loved him anyway and I added my own confirmation and was surprised when his assistant said that she had been telling her boss the same.

I subsequently gave him a copy of C.S. Lewis's book *Mere Christianity.* Has he read it, I wonder?

The nurse on Ward 7 in August 2011 asked if there was anything more I wanted. 'Can you tell me how to get to heaven?'

'Yes,' she said, 'believe in the Lord Jesus Christ.'

Lenka, an attractive Czech nurse, was quite adamant: God wasn't important in her life. All the gods of various religions and sects are confusing – she wasn't bothered about the possibility of meeting God.

Sunday 18th September 2011 evening service at St John's Church Stafford, young people were sharing about their faith in Jesus. Claire, born 28th June 1968 (I had baptised her in Doxey), had come to faith and was an enthusiastic witness for the Lord. It is always encouraging to hear testimonies of what God is doing in other people's lives.

Friday 10th February 2012 a call from NPower about changing services – after talking I said, 'I'm a Christian and I'm going to heaven when I die. Where do you stand?'

'See you there,' he said.

'Praise the Lord!' I replied.

He then told me I was in credit and would receive a cheque – so PTL again!

Still this privilege of talking about Jesus Christ continues; family members, a school friend, a ticket operative at London's Euston Station and a fellow traveller on the 14.07 train to Stafford over the weekend 5th–8th April 2013 could all bear testimony to my evangelising, as does the interruption since writing the word 'evangelising' a few words back in this sentence. The doorbell rang and Paul Gascoigne (not the footballer!), a young twenty-five-year-old man was touting his wares. Purchasing some cleaning materials I also prayed with him that Jesus would become real to him; he gave me permission to include him in these memoirs! But back to 5th–8th April 2013.

This weekend I shared with my nieces and sister-in-law and Matthew my great-nephew about the love of God.

Séances for them appear to be more interesting! Sunday lunch with Jewish and school friends of seventy years ago gave opportunity to speak of the God of Abraham, Isaac and Jacob who led His people through the Red Sea long ago. The African lady at Euston Station ticket office responded to my 'Do you know that Jesus Christ died on the cross for you?' with a definite 'Yes I do.' On the 14.07 train to Stafford my fellow traveller said he was in the property regeneration business. 'I'm in regeneration also,' I said. 'Regeneration of life. Jesus said, "You must be born again."' It transpired that the property man's partner had left the property business to become a New Testament Church Pastor! 'Give your colleague my Christian greetings,' I said as I left the train at Stafford.

Friday 25th July 2014 Matt Pollard called at 4.30pm representing a company dealing with roof surveys. 'May I ask you a personal question?'

'Yes,' he said.

'Do you know that there is a God who loves you and that Jesus died for you?' Looking slightly perplexed he said he'd been asked that question before. It turned out he had called some months back! Said his uncle (his dad's brother) was a born-again believer. Dad was a Jehovah's Witness.

He accepted a copy of *Memories*, my brother's conversion story. January 20th was his father's and Charlie's birthday date though a different year.

Paramedics called out for Mary on 8th August 2015 asked what work I did. Being a retired clergyman led to a lot of questions about faith. I told them that Jesus still stands at the door and knocks (Revelation 3:20) waiting to come in.

Mark (September 15th), a maintenance man doing refurbishment work in the hospital, sitting on a seat in the hospital grounds – I shared with him the reality of knowing Jesus.

March 19th 2016 'Pete' and 'Ackneyd' two Ethiopians met in town. I prayed with them in the street; a lady passing by heard, stopped and shared; she was a Methodist training for local preacher status.

Later that day, I was served in a computer shop by a man with a tattooed cross on his arm. We talked about Jesus. 'Do you know anyone who would speak to you like I'm doing?'

'Yes,' he said, 'my nan!'

Thursday 24th I was at Stafford railway station buying a ticket for Eve Acres' funeral. Speaking about the resurrection, did the office lady really believe what happened? Her grandmother did who had recently lost her husband.

March 10th 2018 I left a copy of *Hope* magazine in a stationery shop, the question 'Who do you say I am?' (about Jesus) on the front.

November 2018 in Markus's hardware shop corner of St Thomas's Street, Stafford, I was talking with a customer about Jesus dealing with rubbishy lives. 'He'd need a bloody big skip to deal with me.'

I explained that Jesus has a BBS; the cross dealt with it all. He who was 'made sin' means that He has the capacity to deal with the most polluted life, but we must chuck our rubbish His way.

We've lived on Tixall Road since 1989. Seeking to be good neighbours Christmas and Easter greetings have been given. Over the years gifts of books such as *The Servant Queen and the King She Serves* (celebrating the Queen's ninetieth birthday), *God's Smuggler* or *Mere Christianity* have been given. Also Kendal mint cake and a large apple or some asparagus from my allotment. Warm responses greet us when calling. We continue in prayer for them.

So I continue to witness as and when, handing out copies of *Love Stafford* (copies of John's Gospel) anticipating seeing results of sowing the seed of God's word. One sows, another waters, but God gives the increase.

The latest opportunity was Thursday 23rd May 2019 on MEP polling day; the three ladies manning the electors' table willingly received a copy with the comment, 'Chapter 3 verse 16 is a good starter.'

Sheldon Vanauken, American academic, poet and novelist, wrote, 'Far more than exploring darkest Africa in the last century or exploring the Galaxy in centuries to come, death if our faith be not false is the splendid adventure.'[13] I confess, too, that death for me is looked upon as a 'splendid adventure', seeing the results of telling others about Jesus.

Friends will be there I have loved long ago,
Joy like a river around me will flow.
Just to be there and my Saviour to know,
Will through the ages be Glory for me.

Can't wait until I reach the end of the Breakwater!

Trustee: Fulham and South Kensington YMCA

Andrew Forbat had introduced me to the YM shortly after my conversion in 1949. It became my spiritual home, Rob and Evelyn Maltby my mentors. My first talks (sermons) were given at the Sunday evening after-church meetings when up to twenty teenagers gathered together. Notes of a talk given on 12th February 1956 emphasise Heaven–Eternity. I was one of a number given

Fulham YMCA c1952

the opportunity of public speaking. These meetings were followed by a communal meal in the basement.

I became a member in 1950, then a committee member in 1960. Invited to be a trustee in 1967 it has been a privilege and blessing to be involved with the development of the work since the 1960s. With Martin McCauley, Paul Laffey, Andrew Maltby, Joel Shepherd, David Griffiths, Martin Hartigan, Jonathan McDowell, Jeff Shepherd, Ivor Sowton, and Jonathan and Marina, it has been a wonderful committee of godly Christian members, a joy to work with and to rejoice in the ministry of youth workers who are supported from the YMCA funds. The advent of Springboard (a leasing group providing accommodation for graduates working in London), the rent obtained used to finance youth workers in over twelve different churches, mainly in the Fulham area. A bungalow was purchased in Tonbridge, Kent for the use of Faith and Joy Maltby, widow and daughter of Robert Maltby who was secretary manager of the YM for over thirty-seven years.

Currently (2019) the work continues apace. Jonathan, my son, has taken on the mantle of trusteeship I vacated in 2017.

Permission to Officiate

The other interest with opportunity for service is Permission to Officiate in the diocese of Lichfield; an annual letter from the diocesan bishop granting authority to individual retired clergy who wish to continue taking services, officiating at weddings, baptisms and funerals. Although officially retired in 1999, I have continued to take services, especially during a vacancy between incumbents coming to a Parish.

One particular blessing, having served as a curate in Carlisle diocese, is the largesse which comes from The Geoffrey and Alice Bennett Trust for the benefit of retired clergy who served in that diocese. A welcome Christmas gift of £75 and other payments to meet unexpected costs are greatly appreciated. Thank God for the generosity and foresight of benefactors.

So my walk along the breakwater of life continues. Now in my 90th year and 60th wedding anniversary year, it is fascinating to contemplate the span of my life, how God has been guiding, directing, forming this piece of clay, moulding it into the vessel He has in mind. What really makes me tick? Who am I? What is the end of man? George O'Brien, Ordinary Chaplain, God's Mate?

....

[13] Sheldon Vanauken *Under the Mercy* (Ignatius Press, 1988)

CHAPTER 9

What Makes Me Tick? Psychology and All That

*'For you have been my hope, Sovereign LORD, my confidence since my youth
. . . you brought me forth from my mother's womb.'*
(Psalm 71:5–6 NIV)

· · · · · · ·

'Know thyself'

(Inscription in the Temple of Apollo in Delphi)

· · · · · · ·

I'm walking on my own along this part of the breakwater. This will be more introspective. Not that I find it disturbing to consider questions like 'Who am I?' 'Where did I come from?' 'Where am I going?' 'What is the meaning of life?' These deep, profound questions have always fascinated me. Now in my eighties I am still intrigued by such questions though that 'blessed assurance' of faith undergirds everything. 'I know whom I have believed, and am persuaded that He is able to keep that which I have committed unto Him' through all eternity (2 Timothy 1:12).

I recall a fellow Clifton student saying, 'We all ought to see a psychiatrist some time during our life.' However, the intriguing, fascinating contemplation of past years, events and attitudes still intrigues me. Why, as a ten-year-old when I had gathered up dust and ashes from the kitchen floor in my boyhood home, did I then scatter them back across the cleaned floor? What trait in my personality made me do it? Also, decade's later destroying long-saved papers, photographs and other memorabilia in my forties? These and other experiences I record, though I am aware that some details, too sensitive, should be omitted or at least euphemistically referred to!

Pictures, visions and unexpected incidents are part of my experience. That vision in Stratton Methodist Sunday school of a white-robed person serving God. A vivid memory of returning home from school in Redan Street, London W14 clutching a Coronation mug of King George VI. In 1947 looking into a courtyard from a toilet in Du Cane Road Hospital, wondering what life was all about. Three incidents at different stages of my life. Reading *Joshua* by F.B. Meyer on top of a Number 11 bus going to work in Finsbury Square in 1958 and thinking, 'Where is my life heading?' Being challenged with 'Dignify the least task with the greatness of your response' meaning, do well the present job you're in!

One of the first philosophical books I bought (1949/50) was *Man's Search for Reality* (5 shillings from Lyon's bookshop). Years later, 2011, Jonathan Sacks' *The Great Partnership – God and the Search for Meaning* indicate the parameters of my ongoing interest in philosophical things. It is good to consider, to contemplate the meaning of life: 'Who am I?' Where did I come from?' 'Where am I heading?' How many do so? A hymn from YM days:

> *Have you any room for Jesus,*
> *He who bore your load of sin?*
> *As He knocks and asks admission,*
> *Sinner, will you let Him in?*

What Makes Me Tick? Psychology and All That

> *Room for pleasure, room for business,*
> *But for Christ, the Crucified,*
> *Not a place that He can enter,*
> *In the heart for which He died?*

Do we really consider our ultimate destiny? 'The Preacher' (Ecclesiastes 12:1 NIV) says, 'Remember your Creator in the days of your youth, before the days of trouble come and the years approach when you will say, "I find no pleasure in them."' I have always been aware of the 'end of life' and look forward with great anticipation to death, not the process of dying but what Vanauken called 'the splendid adventure', of one day knowing 'even as I am fully known' (1 Corinthians 13:12) or as, C.S. Lewis says, when '"the real world" fades away and the Presence in which you have always stood becomes palpable, immediate, and unavoidable'.[14]

Even as I write, I sense the mysterious wonder of it all.

But this chapter purposes to spell out experiences I've had rather than ones to come. What made that ten-year-old boy rake out the fireplace, put ashes in the dustpan, sweep clean the kitchen then cast all the debris back across the newly swept floor? Was it some built-up frustration? Or, more confusingly, trying to deal with my bodily functions in a disgusting way; too embarrassing even seventy years later to record?

Sex and Sexuality

Growing up into teenage years was somewhat traumatic. I was becoming aware of myself, my sexuality. Mum and Dad never breathed a word about the 'birds and bees' and there was no such thing as school sex lessons – you had to make your own way into and around the whole question of sex and where babies came from.

Boys growing up discover their bodies. Sleeping in the same bed Charlie and I discovered that we had penises and pretended that we knew how babies were made. So we, Charlie and I, learnt as we went along. Silly jokes about 'cucumbers growing in greenhouses'. We sang songs such as 'Roll me over in the clover, lay me down and do it again' although uncertain about what 'it' was. 'We're up to number one and the story's just began' sounded interesting without much comprehension, just a growing awareness of another aspect of life other than playing cowboys-and-Indians!

Self-abuse as it was called caused me much heartache. On my way to the pictures one Saturday afternoon I found a magazine, I remember the exact place, which was mildly erotic by today's standards but stirred my imagination. Seventy years later the phrase 'the soft round curve of her breast' comes to mind. The famous cartoon lady 'Jane' in the *Daily Mirror* was always losing her clothes and being seen in her underwear stirred up emotions. So sex, sexuality, has been the one area of my life which has caused much trouble and heartache. Money, wealth, prestige, power, preferment, ambition, cars, exotic holidays do not worry or concern me one bit. But sex – now that's different! And I think, because of experiences in hospital. Reading books, looking at magazines, my inmost personality had become tainted, polluted. Had some 'unclean spirit' caused distress, along the lines of *Screwtape Letters* by C.S. Lewis? I was gloriously released through the ministry of the Rev. Roy Jeremiah of the London Healing Mission in 1971 with the gift of tongues by the baptism in the Holy Spirit. The twenty-first century is reaping the whirlwind of sexual laxity and exploitation. Sadly, amongst teachers, football trainers and some clergy, abuse happens. 'He gave them their requests and sent leanness to their souls.'

Depression, too, dogged my earlier life. Two short notes written in July and August 1961 (which didn't get destroyed) record: *'Depression: what a horrible dreadful thing it is. I've been subject to it for the past few days. It has been no new experience – I've been the victim of it often before. It's dark and frightening. Cold and vicious.'* I spell out in more detail how it affected me. Then a note added 14th February 2006 says, 'I see this happened during my call to the ministry – was I being attacked by the devil and wasn't aware?'

I obviously wasn't sharing with anyone, even Mary!

Homosexuality

Homosexuality is commonplace in the twenty-first century. 'Gay' has lost its historic meaning of lively, bright, playful, happy and full of fun to become the defining word for homosexual orientation. Homosexuality has played its part in my life: boys discovering their private parts is one thing; to have adults being interested in them is different. The incident in the shippen of Farmer Jordan's farm was followed by further incidents years later.

Barnes Common is a large public area of wooded land the other side of Hammersmith Bridge over the River Thames. It was a frequent haunt of the Faroe Road gang: Frank Greenfield, Ron Jordan, Arthur Curtis, Charlie and me. A Sunday-afternoon bus ride over Hammersmith Bridge transported us to the Common, where we roamed and played. One particular occasion saw me disenchanted; leaving the group I decided to return home a short bus ride.

Foolishly I caught the right bus going in the wrong direction; even changing buses didn't help for I needed to cross the road and go in the opposite direction! Eventually I arrived in Leatherhead about fourteen miles outside London in Surrey. A young man took a tearful eleven-year-old to the police station; a Bobby from Hammersmith station was duly sent to inform the O'Brien family that their 'lost' son was safe and well and would be returning home the next day. By now it was late in the evening and the young man kindly offered his parents' home as a refuge to the lost traveller. The police thought this was a happy solution to the problem – there were no safeguarding concerns in those days. I was made welcome and given food by the man's parents. Their home, a two-bedroom terrace, had no guest room and so I shared the young man's bed – which was fine except for the exploring hand which made its presence felt more than once through the night!

I arrived back at Faroe Road not too traumatised from my adventures and with more pocket money through the generosity of the good Samaritans. However, homosexuality was to have a more dramatic and traumatic role in my life. My first experience of hospital life happened in 1947 when pleurisy took me into Du Cane Road Hospital for several weeks. Bed bound, experiencing 'bed baths' by attractive nurses was all right; being educated into the more erotic side of life with 'post cards' by the older men in the thirty-bed Florence Nightingale ward also seemed exciting. Being encouraged to swallow a tube for stomach fluid extraction was less painful than the needle inserted into my pleural cavity, which connected to a tube and a two-way tap switched one way to drain off the accumulated fluid and another way to deposit the fluid into the receiving basin.

After some weeks of fluid extractions, good food and rest, I got better and the doctor (I remember his name to this day) took kindly to me, interviewing me in Sister's office. 'And when did you begin to become a man?' took me by surprise; I had become aware of my body and I must have flushed because a nurse noticing made some jocular remark.

If that had been all then the following would not have happened. The doctor kindly suggested that I might care to visit his private surgery after my hospital discharge.

Trustingly one evening I went to his apartment where he gave me a thorough medical examination, so comprehensive that spread naked on his couch I became vulnerable to his abusive manipulations. An invitation for me to reciprocate the action was declined. I never went back for further examinations.

Another experience was a charming, good looking Irish man, who prayed beautifully: 'The lines have fallen unto us in pleasant places, yea we have a goodly heritage.' We met in 1953 working in the Evangelical Alliance office. Preparations were going ahead for the visit of American evangelist Billy Graham for a twelve-week campaign at Harringay Arena. We took to each other – some personalities do blend – yet his orientation was different. He bought me a Bible, invited me to dinner and was very attentive, a gentle hand up my trouser leg, but no propositions. Many years later as Mary and I walked across Waterloo Bridge he spotted me, stopped his car, warmly greeted me and disappeared out of my life.

How to deal with the 'elephant in the room' occupies the mind of the Church of England still with bishops and other clergy having same-sex partners, some being 'married'.

I was called to task by a couple of gay men over a sermon I preached in December 2002. Matters continued in St John's with a meeting with Bishop Gordon in May 2009 where a frank but not deeply biblical discussion was held. Sadly some members subsequently left St John's. The issue has still not been resolved in the Church of England nor in the country at large, though politicians and academics are seeking to be 'inclusive'.

So What Makes Me?

What experiences have moulded my life? I have very contented memories of home life in Faroe Road; my mother and father stayed together until death parted them. They were straightforward down-to-earth people, honest, hardworking and caring for their family. I never heard them argue, shout or swear at each other. Charlie and I would occasionally rile my father – refusing to go to sleep so he would come down to our bedroom and whack the bedclothes with his belt – but he never laid his hands upon us. The weekly penny (less than the 1p today) was eagerly received and spent at the local sweetshop.

My parents were not overly demonstrative. My father would occasionally playfully tickle or cuddle my mother; we didn't hug or kiss them. It was only after I became a Christian when I was sixteen that I started to greet my mother with a kiss. I cannot recall ever kissing my father, though one memory of his emotional side stands out. During my ten-month stay in Highwood Hospital Sanatorium in 1947 he visited once (Mother and Charlie came regularly). Sitting at the bottom of my bed I was overawed when I saw him near to tears. I treasure that moment, as I do the time when he was ill at home in 1963 and I gave him a bed bath. The memory of his jacket hanging on the kitchen door after his death is poignant.

Some years back, in 2014 to be precise, I sent out a 'round robin' to some dozen or so people asking them to comment on what they thought 'conspired to mould and fashion the George O'Brien you think you know'! I received some interesting replies.

People's Impression Upon First Meeting Me

David Griffiths, a long-standing friend from the 1950s Fulham YMCA days, recalls me 'as someone who could wear a £5 suit and it would look like a £20 suit'. He also remembers the Saturday morning open-air meeting in North End Road market where we witnessed and preached the gospel of Jesus's love.

David Barker, whom I counselled at Harringay, became a political activist as an agent for Norman St John-Stevas. Myra Leslie Carlisle speaks of my 'gentle leading and patience leading us to Jesus'. David Stanbury, a canvasser for the labour party, was impressed that the 'vicar' called. He had no 'Damascene moment' then but later came to faith in the Salvation Army in Plymouth, Devon.

Being a Minister

Joan, a long-standing member of St Thomas's Church, says, 'You were easy to talk to . . . having a blast of new ideas and openly Christian . . . with joy in your voice when you speak of the Lord.'

Trevor Partington, an Elim pastor, speaks with affection of our meeting in 1968, when a Pentecostal and an Anglican 'discovered that there was a spiritual affinity. With David Taylor (Baptist pastor who was appointed to Stafford), the three of us became very close'.

Pat and George Doyle were married in February 1965. Pat remembers Mary holding our newborn baby Marina as they walked down the aisle. Pat has memories of being welcomed at Doxey Vicarage after a rain-filled camping holiday and being blessed with the Holy Spirit after prayer.

William Parker moved to Stafford in 1982, with 'seek first My kingdom' on his heart from the Lord: find a church first, then a place to live! He found Doxey church 'and I felt immediately welcomed and at home'. The next day at a local estate agent's, he enquired about a one-bedroom flat. 'We've just had one come in, sir, but the particulars haven't been printed yet.' 'It's got to be in Doxey.' It was, and William made an offer which was accepted that lunchtime.

I had the joy of marrying William and Jan, even wearing a brand-new dog collar for the occasion!

And then dear Mary Herbert who, metaphorically speaking, said after her conversion that she was 'Camping out at Calvary'. Our meaningful relationship started as 'A vicar with no church and a church with no vicar and a camel out in front'. I married Mary's daughter Jayne because the vicar was away on holiday. Mary was challenged by 'the Almighty and He is always right'. She gave in. 'I prayed, "I've got it wrong, can I start again with you?" He said yes.'

Theology and Doctrine

Two friends spoke about belief. Doug Grounds, a schoolteacher and valued member of Doxey Church wrote:

> *I think two things about you stand out among these recollections. The first is the confident, sure, biblical faith which was the hallmark of your ministry among us. While some, including me, struggled at times over the mismatch between scriptural certainties and one's experience of life, you seemed to go blithely on. The second is your friendly, down-to-earth personality, so that you always seemed to come up with a smile after the stickiest PCC meeting or whatever.*
>
> *One particular memory is of the occasion you brought a serving prisoner – I think his name was John – to the assembly you were taking at Walton School. It caused quite a stir in various ways, but the pupils ever after looked forward to your assemblies.*

Another long-standing friend, Geoff, wrote:

> *Our friend George is a Conservative Evangelical Christian whose faith proceeds from a place of absolute truth, namely Jesus. This stance is in irresolvable conflict with our aim in our conversations with him, to plead that words and language do not have a fixed meaning as a moment's reflection on the words 'see 'and 'view' will show. All religion in our opinion depends upon one's suppositions*

and hypotheses and it is a disservice to Christianity not to see that. And so it has worked out, notwithstanding George's willingness to read outside the narrow literature of his sect and to discuss with humour and passion the conflicts he sees but does not believe. His point of view appears to remain unshaken. He is a permanent Bartimaeus continuing on the Way. So what is also good about our friendship is its basis in very similar experiences when young and marrying and in many ways a common mind pleasure in discussions of faith and shared interests in gardens and DIY and accountancy, etc. but above all for us his ministry at Doxey Church which continued to us when he moved into chaplaincy work and eventual retirement.

Finally a comment from a Probus friend, Martin, which I treasure: *'You are not sanctimonious'!*

Two questionnaires from some 'counsellor training' conference I attended have revealing answers: 'One thing I would like to change about myself' was 'to stop picking my finger'. My mother constantly picked at her right hand index finger, and I inherited the same peculiarity. Though now I'm able to discuss it! Being aware of my own shortcomings or idiosyncrasies helps me to appreciate other people's problems.

Years ago I received a letter which said. 'You always were a bit of a John Blunt.' The comment made me think. Yes I do at times make the odd caustic remark. I suppose if the Yorkshire people can 'call a spade a spade' a Londoner can be forthright. But words can be hurtful and remembered. I was told when apologising for a remark I'd made, 'It's not the first time'!

I have crossed swords with a number of people, interestingly over such things as choice of hymns or style of music! By and large I consider that I'm a fairly integrated person; aware of my faults and failings, yet having that confidence that God knows me better than I know myself, and that there is nothing that He and I are not talking about.

It is fascinating to consider that temptation is always around.
'Prone to wander Lord I feel it,
Prone to leave the God I love,
Take my heart, Lord, take and seal it
Seal it from thy throne above'.

But I know that humanly speaking I am getting near to the end of the breakwater. What is the water like there? Is it deep? What is there across that vast expanse? I live with great anticipation and expectancy of what is yet to be, I shall see Him face to face and tell the story 'Saved by Grace'.

....

[14] CS Lewis *Mere Christianity* (Harper Collins, 2017)
copyright © CS Lewis Pte Ltd 1942

CHAPTER 10

Allotment, Probus, Poetry, Books, Sermons and Heaven

'It is since Christians have largely ceased to think of the other world that they have become so ineffective in this. Aim at Heaven and you will get earth "thrown in": aim at earth and you will get neither.'[15]

• • • • • • • •

'But I know that humanly speaking I am getting near to the end of the breakwater. What is the water like there? Is it deep? What is there across that vast expanse? I live with great anticipation and expectancy of what is yet to be, I shall see Him face to face and tell the story 'Saved by Grace'.

I have often said 'If I die', which makes people think or say, 'What do you mean "If I die"?' Everyone will eventually die – it's a one-to-one certainty! Indeed, that has certainly been the case thus far but it doesn't take into account that the Bible says that 'we who are still alive' (1 Thessalonians 4:15,17) at 'the coming of the Lord'. The 'second coming of the Lord' teaching is what makes the difference. It's a promise we should be aware of and prepared for.

Humanly speaking I am getting near the end of the breakwater, I can see rocks and waves which indicate that that 'last scene of all, which ends this strange eventful history' is getting nearer; '*sans* teeth (I need a denture), *sans* eyes (I need glasses), *sans* taste, sans everything'.

Everything could be nearer than I think. Is the end of the breakwater in sight? Whatever, there is still that 'splendid adventure' of going through death which Vanauken speaks about in *Under the Mercy*.

What memories will I leave behind? Indeed what would I wish to be remembered for? Some years ago I read that 'writing your own obituary focuses you to look back upon your life and look forward to your future destiny'. So I did!

George's Obituary

> *With regret we record the death of George O'Brien of Tixall Road. George, with his wife Mary and three children, lived in Stafford since 1968.*
>
> *In 1968 George came to Stafford to be the vicar of St Thomas's Church, Castletown with Doxey. He saw the building of Doxey Church, which was opened in 1975.*
>
> *After twenty years in Parochial Ministry George left Doxey to become full-time chaplain at St George's Hospital with Kingsmead and worked on the General side at the old SGI and the new Stafford General Hospital.*
>
> *George was well known in Stafford and his ecumenical ministry embraced all denominations – he used to say that he had preached in every Orthodox church in Stafford save for the Strict Brethren and the Quakers.*
>
> *He had a reputation for always talking about going to Heaven; one day the Church NB*

sported a newspaper cutting declaring that a Mr O'Brien and a Miss Heaven had announced their engagement!

George wrote his memoirs just before he died. It was entitled A Walk on the Breakwater with 'God's Mate' and an 'Ordinary Chaplain'. George leaves his wife Mary after fifty-five years of marriage, a daughter Marina, training for the Ministry, and two married sons David and Jonathan and two grandchildren Isaac and Amy.

George will be remembered as a faithful servant of God, honoured as a man of faith who sort to proclaim the gospel of Christ – although he himself would say that whatever people thought of him and his reputation he was accountable to God 'who knows me better than I know myself'. May he 'Rest in Peace and Rise in Glory'.

But I am still here, alive and active, with what interests, hopes, fears or anticipations? What is my 'bucket list'?

- Staying close to Jesus.

- Nurturing and developing faith through Bible reading, prayer and meeting with other Christians.

- Hopefully seeing these memoirs finished in print.

- Mary enjoying a new hip replacement June 18th 2019!

- Continuing supportive ministry at St John's Church Littleworth.

- Still being an evangelist spreading the good news about Jesus.

- Seeing my brother's family coming to believe in Jesus.

- Having a stairway access into the loft area at 185, Tixall Road! The loft area of our house has occupied a lot of my spare time and has often frustrated Mary! I still maintain that to have the stairs extended into the loft instead of the 1930s magnificent loft ladder facility (a dream antique acquisition!) would provide better access and add value to the property.

Apart from this 'bucket list', several other areas have occupied my time and interest.

Allotment

For some 15 years I had an Avon Rise alotment plot. It was good relating to other plot holders and enjoy a fruitful activity. Steve Mellor ably manages the site. When I retired two years ago, he presented me with a mug inscribed 'And on the 8th Day God created GARDENING'. I am now an honorary member of the Avon Rise Allotments.

Probus

Professional and Business, a club for retired men. The name is derived from the first three letters of each word Pro-Bus; some wag has said 'Prostate Removed Other Bits Under Surveillance'!

I was introduced to the Stafford branch (it's a country-wide organisation) by Bob Button, a retired school teacher. The monthly luncheon meetings with a visiting speaker were very amiable, keeping me in touch with a whole range of people from fascinating backgrounds of influence and expertise: engineers, teachers, scientists, policemen. I was with them for twenty-one years serving on the committee as Almoner, Vice Chair and Chairman. Being for much of the time the only Clergyman member I was occasionally asked to conduct funeral services. My years walking along the breakwater with Probus members were very delightful and fulfilling ones.

Poetry

Those poems on the pottery in Hamvale which I committed to memory are the very first beginnings of verse which I enjoy, doggerel as well as more serious material.

At school Miss Jackson, our English teacher, encouraged us with Shakespeare's 'All the world's a stage, and all the men and women merely players.' Some pieces I know by heart, many bits are snippets. A.P. Lord Wavell whose book *Other Men's Flowers* contains poems he could 'repeat entire or in great part', is one of a number of poetry books I have (I should dip into them more!).

One particular area of verse is the vast amount of hymnology. I am so grateful for the Stratton and Bush Methodist chapels I went to during evacuation days where I first sang about 'The Old, Old story of Jesus and His love'. I know many more hymns by heart than I do other poetry. I use many verses when praying. Jim Packer also likes hymns, quoting twenty-nine verses in his book *Knowing God*. Over the years a number of friends have gone into verse about me, my family and ministry – Peter Price and Doreen Bennett, they continue some fascinating insights which I hope you'll be able explore in the Addendum. I went into verse with Bob Ben-Nathan one Christmas/Hanukkah which you'll see there.

Books

Books are also part of my life. The *Waverley Thorndike English Dictionary*, two volumes purchased in 1948, are a special joy and well used. Books given, books recommended, books as prizes have given much joy. Although some three or four years back I reduced my considerable library by half, thinking that, should I die (sic), it would help the family with the decision, 'What shall we do with George's books!

From that early memory at school engrossed in the book to the oblivion of the teachers call, I have found delight and whiled away hundreds of hours reading books. I think it was George Carey, ex-Archbishop of Canterbury, who said he reads fifty pages a day. In my eighties I still love reading: theological works, Bible commentaries, dictionaries, DIY books, arts, painting, drawing, philosophy. Particular favourites, read, reread and many underlined and annotated are:

- Dale Carnegie *Public Speaking and Influencing Men in Business*
- Arnold Bennett *How to Live on 24 Hours a Day*
- Handley Moule *Life In Christ*
- F.B. Meyer *Joshua and the Land of Promise*
- Jim Packer *Knowing God*
- Dr Martyn Lloyd-Jones *Faith on Trial: Psalm 73*
- John Stott *Your Confirmation, The Cross of Christ and Essentials*
- Charles Handy books

These are just some of the books and authors I enjoy and profit from. A special mention of Nabeel Qureshi's *Seeking*

Allah Finding Jesus: A Devout Muslin Encounters Christianity, for anyone wanting to understand Islam.

One particular book an anthology of C.S. Lewis's books, *The Business of Heaven*, given as a Christmas present in 2001 by Sue Savage has been read daily ever since. And I have come belatedly but enjoyably to Charles Dickens.

Sermons

What a profound and glorious privilege it has been, still is, to preach 'the unsearchable riches of Christ'. I have already mentioned that opportunities to speak at the Fulham YMCA after-church meetings gave me the initial grounding in public speaking. Another book, *Heralds of God* by James S. Stewart has been instructive: '"I came into town," wrote John Wesley, "and offered them Christ."' Could any life work be more thrilling or momentous? With prayer, prayerful preparation and the Holy Spirit's enabling, the 'Ministry of the Word' has been done I trust to the glory of God and a blessing to the hearers.

'No man,' declared James Denny, 'can give at once the impression that he himself is clever and that Jesus Christ is mighty to save.' I have discovered that something (someone – the Holy Spirit) seems to enable the preaching of prayerfully prepared sermons or talks. Especially relevant has been funeral orations with appropriate visual illustrations or comments. Even a *'sod off'* comment was well received on one occasion! Here are some favourite re-used sermons

• On the Mountain with Abraham and Isaac

• Three Nautical Flags: P (Blue Peter), G and H

- God's Basket (courtesy of Trevor Lloyd)
- The Prodigal Son: his Sadness, his Madness, his Gladness (courtesy David Pawson)
- The Advantage of Knowing Christ, the Adventure of Living for Christ, the Anticipation of Being with Christ
- What an X can mean: it's wrong; a kiss; a direction sign

Heaven

Hebrews 11:10 records that 'Abraham looked for a city which has foundations whose maker and builder is God'.

Eternity: the end of the world, the beginning of a new earth and a new heaven. The recognition that Jesus Christ is King of kings and Lord of lords; that one day every knee shall bow and every tongue confess that Jesus Christ is Lord. These are the thoughts which govern my life and inform my philosophy.

At times I surprise myself – 'Do I really believe all this?'

Yes, I really do; I am so looking forward to 'knowing as I am known' (1 Corinthians 13:12).

Chris Wright, in his book *The God I Don't Understand*, adds a further dimension. He speaks about his delight at being in the British Library, surrounded by the millions of books which encapsulate the 'accumulated learning, wisdom, wit, and literature of multiple civilisations and languages' and wonders how long it would take to 'absorb and enjoy' it all. 'Think of the prospect! All human culture, language, literature, art, music, science, business, sport, technological achievement – actual and potential – all available to us. All of it with the poison of evil and sin sucked out of it forever. All of it glorifying God.

All of it under his loving and approving smile. All of it for us to enjoy with God and indeed being enjoyed by God. And all eternity for us to explore it, understand it, appreciate it, and expand it.'[16]

The Church of England report 'The Mystery of Salvation' has 'Human destiny in Heaven, will be an everlasting participation, in the exploration of the inexhaustible riches of the Divine nature'.

The best is yet to be and all manner of things are yet to be.

A glorious vista as I contemplate the end of the breakwater.

Have you found this walk interesting?

Will you be there with me at its climax?

If you are unsure of your own walk you could pray.

You could use the words my brother said on page 108:
"*Jesus, I need you. Come into my heart.*"

Or say something like this:

"*O God, thank you that you desire to walk with me.
Forgive me for going my own way.
Help me to know your presence in the rest of my life's journey.
In Jesus' Name, Amen.*"

And now tell someone what you've done!

....

[15] CS Lewis *Mere Christianity* (Harper Collins, 2017) © CS Lewis Pte Ltd 1942|
[16] Christ Wright *The God I Don't Understand: Reflections on Tough Questions of Faith* (Zondervan, 2008)

ADDENDUM

Both the Jewish and Christmas celebrations coincide. Bob Ben-Nathan had sent greetings for Hanukkah and Christmas. This made me go into verse as follows:

For Jew and Gentile both alike
We celebrate together.

To Abraham our mutual one
The Promise was forever
That Jews and Gentiles will abide
Within one fold together.

So celebrate our mutual faith
The mystery that will sever
The enmity and lostness
The fallenness for ever.

For Christ has come
The Promised One
To Abraham and nation(s)
Who brings us Peace and Righteousness
And is for all – Salvation

Other verses written at different times by different people continue to delight.

On 3rd July 2008 we shared a meal with John and Susan Corcoran, and Doreen and Roy Bennett to celebrate 40 years since I was inducted as Vicar of St Thomas's Church.

An Ode to George
by Doreen Bennett

Forty years ago today
A bright young vicar came the way
Of Castletown and Doxey

He brought with him Mary – a lovely young wife
And Marina and David to start a new life –
At the vicarage at Doxey

His intention was to spread the Word
Through Bible and prayer to those who'd not heard
Of the love of our Lord
And His death on the cross
That sins were forgiven
Because of this loss

Along with this vision
There'd been the decision
To build a new church – at Doxey
Where new estates and houses old
Would increase numbers to our fold
And fill each seat (there was no pew)
In our church so big and new – at Doxey

St Andrew's (our sister church) in hut so small
Combined with St Thomas's items to install
While Venables and Universal too
Asked what their firms could do

What were our needs; what was our want?
They kindly provided lectern, chairs and font
In our church – at Doxey

George supervised this mammoth task
Through rain and mud, so much to ask
There with camera was our friend,
Who recorded events right to the end
Services took place both outside and in
On the church carpark and the 'building of tin'
The bishop came at our behest
And the church of St Thomas and St Andrew was blessed
At Doxey

While all this was going on
The vicar and Mary produced a new son – called Jonathan
The youngest of three, it turned out to be,
The ideal family at Doxey

For twenty years George worked to establish the church
Worship, home groups, missions, baptisms, weddings,
so rare
And not forgetting his pastoral care
All of this a vicar's lot – at Doxey

At his side all the while,
With a beautiful smile was Mary
Wife, mother – and to all a friend
She did so much to extend
The love of our Lord – at Doxey

Always a very capable cook
She encouraged us all to write a book
Of recipes with Bible tales
For which we had so many sales
To help with the work – at Doxey

A duty George took diligently
Was as chairman of the PCC!
Through decisions large and small
Finance, buildings, worship, and all
Sometimes he had to take control
And suggested we had a poll – at Doxey

Dear George decided to retire
But the congregation still admire
The path he trod
As a man of God – at Doxey

The knowledge, love and skills he knew
Have taken him to pastures new
St George's – a mental hospital where
He helped to heal minds which were not aware
Of the blessings from our Lord above
To everyone who seeks His love

We wish you well, through God's good grace
And hope you'll still keep up the pace
A swim each day to keep so agile
And lovely grandchildren who make you smile

So now, dear George, we often ponder
'When the roll is called up Yonder'
That you'll be there –
This we know
'Cause you love our Saviour so!

....

In a lovely provision of 'nursing care' Carol (name changed) was able to attend a church group at Brunel Manor. It became her spiritual blessing.

Ode to Brunel

It was in a place in Devon at a manor called Brunel,
I was sitting in the garden, there was a wood smoke smell,
And then from out the darkness, the Lord, He came to me,
It was a very special feeling, one I thought I'd never see.

There was no sound, there was no light,
Only the darkness of that night,
I was alone with the bench that I sat upon,
And then suddenly together with the Lord as one.

I didn't understand it; it was all so new to me,
But since that night at the manor, I have been able to see,
That it wasn't God who stayed away, because I was full of sin,
It was me, myself who couldn't or wouldn't let Him in.

I feel that I have had a weight lifted off my shoulder,
I'm glad I've found this special peace
before I got much older,

I suppose that I was always frightened to admit
that He was there
But now I'm proud to accept His love and know
I've got His care.

And so I'm very happy with my Lord, my newfound friend,
And I know, when I get frightened, on Him I can depend,
I think I've made a start on the mount of communication,
And my heart is full of joy and the greatest adoration.

And so dear George and Mary, I say this from the heart,
That those days with you in Devon gave me
a brand-new start,
In itself it was a miracle, how I came to be right there,
So I just wanted you to know these things,
and with me the feelings share.

I think that night when you found me crying by the fire,
You knew the tears were not for me but for
one much higher,
I hadn't gone away from you, I'd simply gone to me,
Because I knew the time had come, my God for me to see.

I thank you for your blessing and for understanding me,
Your kindness and your friendship and for
allowing me to see,
That it doesn't have to be dramatic,
there need not be thunder,
For a confused and lost person,
to experience God's wonder.

God bless you.
Carol, 5th July 1995

Peter, who looked after the vicarage whilst we were on holiday, wrote this.

The Holiday Blues

As I sat in the kitchen quite lonely
My thoughts they gently did stray
To the lads who had gone off to Scilly
To have a nice holiday

It was only yesterday morning
That off to the station they went
And I'd waved them away feeling happy
But that happiness now is quite spent

The fact of the whole situation
Is that I miss them about the whole place
Dobs with his drums and electrics
And Jonathan's bright smiling face

Now when they were here I was moaning
About the mess and sink full of plates
And the washing and ironing and dusting
And I said I'd leave them to their fates

But the truth of the matter I'm telling
I enjoyed it all really you know
But I had to pretend to be harassed
But my anger was only for show

So hurry on back you good people
I've missed you so much it's a sin
And there's nowhere to go for a coffee
When you're there on the job – LIVING IN

He wrote on the paper, 'Missing you.' We kept in touch for some years, then nothing.

....

A lovely homemade 'Farewell' card had the following comments:

> *Doxey Church will live on for many, many years and linked firmly with it the name O'Brien. You saw us through our joys and fears and certainly made things happen; but not always as you wished.*
>
> *Your sermons always hit the hearts of 'God's Subjects' gathered there.*
>
> *Perhaps you never knew how much you sometimes hurt the ones who cared. But maybe we forget that vicars are only human too. No-one, George, could ever put across 'God's Word' as well as you. For this you'll always be remembered and you'll be missed so much, of that there is no doubt.*
>
> *And when once more we're all assembled within the arms of Christ where we are all the same, maybe we'll meet – I'll say, 'Hello, Mr O'Brien.' You'll smile, shake my hand, then gently whisper: 'I'm sorry, I've forgotten your name!'*

Charlie's Thoughts at Christmas 2013

A fantasy based upon fact

'Ere, you'll never believe it, but I was down the North End Road last Saturday and I saw Brother George and some blokes from the YMCA just about to shout the odds about God, so I thought I'd stand in a doorway and listen.

Well blow me down, Brother George got on the box and d'ya know, the first thing he said was, 'And it's no use standing in doorways – God knows where you are!' You could 'ave knocked me down with a fevver – I didn't stay very long. That was some years ago in the 50s.

George went on to become a vicar in Stafford an' he was always banging on about how much God loves us. I used to say, 'That's alright, mate. If there is a God, when I meet 'im I'll say, "My bruvver's a vicar in Stafford" – that'll help me.' Dear ole George used to get quite upset and said no it won't do you any good – it's Jesus you need.

But we get on well together and years later, when I'd retired and was living in 'Anwell, he asked me if I'd help out doing some electrics in a Fulham shop. I did and it was great fun.

We rewired the shop – it was known as 'The Fulham Job'. Brother George was in charge and we did a lot of work together, re-wiring, plumbing, and decorating. I'd go for a day and afterwards we enjoyed a drink in The George pub. That was in the 90s!

We (Eileen and I) decided to move to Devon where Helen and Steve were and it was down there that I got this bloody cancer. I tell yer, when yer gets something like that it makes you think; dear old Eileen had been through the hoops wiv it and we managed to get over it – she had a tough time though – the girls were helpful.

I didn't really know what it was all about – didn't really talk about it – went through all the hospital visits and tests but didn't get much better. Brother George came to see me and I remember 'e painted the doors at No.2 when I had to go to the hospital. An' then, of course, we had that visit to Carmarthen; Sue had arranged a time-share exchange in March 2003.

For some reason I wanted Bruvver George to come, an' I remember seeing him and Mary standing outside the railway station wondering where we were. I remember trying to shout but didn't have enough breath – this bloody cancer was making me short of breath. However, he heard me and it was great to see him.

Of course you know what happened on that Tuesday. I'd said to 'im, 'Does it seem selfish now?' Somehow I knew I was going to kick the bucket an' I wanted some sort of help – if you like I wasn't hiding in a doorway any more.

Brother George spoke about blokes who were taken on for a day's work all at different hours of the day. At the end of the day the boss gave them all the same wages. 'Blow me down, that ain't fair – I've slaved me guts out all day long and these blokes 'ave done just one hour and get the same pay!'

And it seemed to me that I was a bit like one of the blokes who'd been taken on at the last hour.

Brother George said God's like that – cos He loves us. And he said, 'All you need to say is, "Jesus I need you, come into my heart."' And I suddenly realised what I needed. I just cried out, 'Jesus, I need you, come into my heart.' Brother George gave me a hug an' prayed something about the Holy Spirit making it real.

Later on I needed to have a slash – Eileen and Sue and Mary and George were sitting in the lounge. I tell yer, I'd been thinking and wondering what had happened. I sort of felt better, more at peace and I said, 'It's all right, I've got George's Jesus; eternal life,' and went back to bed.

The next day we went to the Botanic Gardens where George pushed me around in a wheelchair. For some reason I kept on thinking about things. George and I sang a verse of the hymn we'd learnt in Stratton as evacuee boys and I remember saying, 'My Saviour, I suppose I must have done something right after all.'

And of course you know what happened the next day. Eileen and Sue were with me – they gave me some melon to eat and then the strangest of things happened. I suddenly sensed that something was happening – I looked and seemed to feel *a Presence near, Angels came all around* and I fell asleep in the arms of George's Jesus and woke up here . . . it's amazing and He is – it's wonderful beyond words.

Brother George was always wittering on about Jesus. I remember when I was in the REME he gave me a letter to give to another raving religious bloke who was in my block! I must say this for him, he's consistent. He's still at it – giving books about the Incarnation. I hope you read it cos now I know it's true. As I said before, it's amazing and He is – it's wonderful beyond words. I hope you find out too.

Don't worry about me and have a Happy Jesus Birthday.

Lots of love,

Chas/Dad xxx

....

Support in Stressful Situations

St George's hospital provided a support service to help staff in stressful situations. It so happened that my wife and I had an experience of a stressful situation when we arrived home from Julie Jones's wedding on 28th March 1992 to find our house had been burgled. An uninvited intruder had entered our home.

It was a relatively 'clean job' – no graffiti, no damage – but the loss of a number of items, personal property of sentimental value.

How did we cope?

The shock, the situation, the sympathy

There was the initial shock and then immediately we did three things:

1. We stood in the kitchen and prayed for peace and calm.
2. We put the kettle on for a cup of tea!
3. We phoned the police.

We took stock of the situation – what was missing? The video player, all the CDs, a ring, a silver necklace, my cassock – MY CASSOCK! The cheeky blighters pinched my cassock, the one I was ordained in, the one with the frayed edges and torn lining. It's funny what becomes newsworthy. I suppose it's not every day that a clergyman's gown gets taken – not to wear, but to wrap the loot in and carry it away.

The young policeman who came was sympathetic. We phoned others, our local church, family members. We prayed again, this time amongst the upheaval in our bedroom, that Jesus would take away the taint of the intruder and every room be filled with His presence and light.

Who sets the agenda?

We almost didn't go to church (it was a Sunday) but we thought, 'Why should a thief set our agenda for us?' So we went, half-an-hour late, but the warmth and friendship of our friends there, including the bishop and his wife, brought added peace and comfort.

As news got around, more love and sympathy flowed our way; people called or phoned or wrote – a card from our daughter was a special delight.

Lessons we learned

We discovered a number of things:

>   1. We were not alone – 1,700 other incidents had happened within three months.
>
>   2. The joy of discovering that not everything of value had been taken – a favourite brooch got overlooked, a CD found in the player too.
>
>   3. It was almost worth it for the blessing of friends sharing their love.
>
>   4. Above all, the realisation that life is more important than items of personal possession.

But I still wonder where my cassock is

....

Sermons

Those favourite 're-used' sermons with outline headings.

On the Mountain with Abraham and Isaac

Genesis 22:1–11

God provides from the mountain situation. Five aspects:

> • The Mount of Communication v.1
>   God said, Abraham answered
>   Billy Bray 'Tell Father about it'

- The Mount of Obedience v.3–18
  Trust and obey. 'Whatever he says to you, do it'
  (John 2:5)

- The Mount of Worship v.5
  'We will worship.' Is it the stance of our lives?

- The Mount of Faith v.5b, 8
  'And then we will come back to you'
  'God himself will provide'

- The Mount of Surrender/Sacrifice v.9–10
  'You have not withheld your only son from me'
  Is your all on the altar of sacrifice laid?

....

Three nautical Flags: P (Blue Peter) G and H Loaned by Susan Corcoran

International Code of Signals: three flags P-G-H tell a story.

Mark 4:35–41 Jesus calms the storm.

- Flag P
  Vessel about to set sail. Starting out in life.

- Flag G
  I require a Pilot. Difficult times.

- Flag H
  I have a Pilot on board.
  Have you asked Him to be your Pilot through life?
  Do you want a Pilot? Signal then to Jesus.

God's Basket (courtesy of Trevor Lloyd)

Me in the COOP trolley

Three containers:

- a trug with workman's tools, signifying ability and service

- a basket of fruit, signifying provision, seedtime and harvest

- a shopping trolley named 'God's Basket' – are you in it?

....

The Prodigal Son (courtesy of David Pawson)

Luke 15 'The Lost Son':

- His sadness: he cavilled, he travelled, he revelled

- His madness: he went to the dogs, he lost his togs, he ate with the hogs

- His gladness: he got the seal, he danced the reel, he ate the veal

....

Philippians 3:1–21

- The Advantage of Knowing (or being *in*) Christ (v. 7-8)

- The Adventure of Living for Christ (v. 10-14)
- The Anticipation of Being with Christ (v. 21-23)

What X can mean: it's wrong, a kiss, a direction sign

- When things go wrong: 2 + 2 = 5 X
- Sending a greeting: sealed with a kiss xxx
- A signpost showing direction
- Good Friday's **X** means that wrongs can be forgiven
  The cross shows that love is displayed
- The way of the cross shows the way to go
  Jesus said, 'Follow me.'

....

Doxey Church 40th Anniversary Celebrations

Martin Strang, the vicar, invited us to join in the celebrations and share some thoughts.

Paint Brush and Spanner

One of the first things I did in 1968 was to decorate the inside of St Andrew's Tin Tabernacle. Ossie Lloyd helped with scaffolding from U.V. Grinding Wheel Company.

Secondly, we moved the oak fencing from the pavement and bolted it to concrete posts at the back of the church site. Bill from the Giles caravan site helped.

Mary and I visited some weeks ago. The Tin Tabernacle St Andrew's has gone. At the back there's a wilderness area, a couple of oak posts a reminder of what was. They tell a story of what has happened in the last 40 years.

Firstly, many people, like St Andrew's, have gone. They have gone to be with the Lord: Mrs Allanson, Bob Bailey, Gordon and Gina Baillie, Harold Bee, Gordon Bevans, Tom and Joyce Beach, Ruby Bostock, Rene Calder, Fanny Emberton, Eileen Firman, Elaine Grounds, Kathleen Harrison, John, Monica and Michael Hawkins, Irene Lloyd, John and Hilda Lunt, Geoff and Barbara McKenzie, Tony Nugent, Harry Parrack, Daisy Pye, Colin Parsons and his parents, Reg and Elizabeth Rowland, Edna Revins, Mrs Sharratt, Margaret Stephens, Pam Stanbury, Trixie Whipps, Reg and Edie Weatherer, Allan and Mary Wilson, Mrs Wilson (Jane's mother), Mrs Wostenholme, and Don Young.

It's good to celebrate their memory today.

Secondly, others, like the patch of ground at the back of St Andrew's site, are in a wilderness state. Jesus said to some disciples, 'Will you also go away?' Sadly some for whatever reason are out of fellowship.

Where is the blessedness I knew
When first I saw the Lord?
Where is the soul refreshing view
Of Jesus and His word?

What peaceful hours I once enjoyed!
How sweet their mem'ry still
But they have left an aching void
The world can never fill.

However thirdly, down at the St Andrew's site, all is not lost. The hall behind St Andrew's has been renewed, altered and refurbished and there the Lord is now worshipped by the New Testament Church.

Today we celebrate this purpose-built, furnished and landscaped church costing £66,000 dedicated in March 1975.

In 40 years many from this church have come to faith in Jesus, working as teachers, nurses, engineers, husbands, fathers, wives and mothers.

Some have served as missionaries abroad, four men have been ordained, one consecrated as Bishop.

So today we rejoice.
How good is the God we adore,
Our gracious unchangeable Friend
His love is as great as His power,
And knows neither measure nor end.

'Tis Jesus the First and the Last
Whose Spirit will guide us safe home
We'll praise Him for all that is past
And trust Him for all that's to come.

....

Perhaps the final thought of my 'Walk' could be 'Obedience' by George McDonald (1824–1905). Rob and Evelyn Maltby first introduced me to this poem.

I said, 'Let me walk in the fields,'
He said, 'No, walk in the town.'
I said, 'There are no flowers there,'
He said, 'No flowers, but a crown.'
I said, 'But the skies are black;
There is nothing but noise and din'
And He wept as He sent me back –
'There is more,' He said; 'there is sin.'

I said, 'I shall miss the light,
And friends will miss me they say.'
He answered; 'Choose tonight
If I am to miss you or they.'

I pleaded for time to be given.
He said, 'Is it hard to decide?'
It will not seem so hard in heaven
To have followed the steps of your Guide.'

I cast one look at the fields,
Then set my face to the town;
He said, 'My child, do you yield?
Will you leave the flowers for the crown?'

Then into His hand went mine;
And into my heart came He;
And I shall walk in a light divine,
The path I had feared to see.

The Use of Poetry, Verse and Hymns in my life

Ephesians Chapter 5, vv 18/19 speaking to (yourselves) in psalms, hymns and spiritual songs, sing and make music in your heart to the Lord.

Pages 31 and 137, indicate my fondness for verse. Those two Toby jugs set the trend for my life!.

Different verses recall memories, e.g. Scouting:

"Have you ever watched the camp fire
when the wood has fallen low
And the ashes start to whiten
round the embers crimson glow.
And the night sounds all around you
Making silence doubly sweet
And a full moon above you that the spell may be complete
Tell me, were you ever nearer
To the land of heart's desire
Than when you sat there thinking
With your feet before the fire."

Or a line in Stratton Methodist Church, Sunday School Anniversary.

"Ten lepers came to Him for aid
All outcast and forlorn..."
Hymns of those days ring deep into my soul.
Pass me not O gentle Saviour
Hear my humble cry
While on others thou art calling
Do not pass me by.

From the YM days.

> *Lord of all pots and pans and things*
> *Since I've no time to be*
> *A saint by doing lovely things*
> *Or watching late with thee*
> *Make me a saint, by getting meals*
> *And washing up the plates.*

My personal spiritual life, that close relationship with the Lord Jesus can be expressed and illustrated by verse, poetry and hymns. They are a great treasury of truth.

I use (quote) hymns throughout the day and when I pray.

Early Morning/Daybreak

> *When thou wake 'st in the morning*
> *Ere though tread the unknown way*
> *Of the day that lies before thee*
> *Through the coming busy day*
> *Whether sunbeams promise gladness*
> *Whether dim forebodings fall*
> *Be thy dawning glad or gloomy*
> *Go to Jesus, tell Him all.*

Forgiveness and being "In Christ"

> *'I died in Him, not mine to life suppress*
> *Mine to let Him live out His holiness*
> *Yea to let Him through me His life express*
> *Not I but His*

Holiness of life:

> *"Almighty God, how shall poor wretches brook*
> *Thy dreadful look" Able an heart of iron to appal…*
> *When Thou shalt call for every man's peculiar book*
> *What others mean to do I know not well,*
> *Yet I hear tell that some would turn Thee to some leaves therein*
> *So void of sin, that they in merit shall excel*
> *But I resolve, when Thou shalt call for mine*
> *That to decline, and thrust a Testament into Thy hand*
> *Let that be scanned.*
> *There Thou wilt find my faults are Thine!*
> *Amen.*
>
> *George Herbert (Judgement 1633)*

Accusations of the Devil:

> *When Satan tempts me to despair*
> *And tells me of the guilt within*
> *Upward I look and see Him there*
> *Who made an end of all my sin.*
> *Because the sinless Saviour died*
> *My sinful soul is counted free*
> *For God the just is satisfied*
> *To look on Him and pardon me.*

The Hope of Heaven

O that will be glory for me glory for me
When by His grace
I shall look on is face
That will be glory be glory for me.
When the roll is called up yonder I'll be there
Friends will be there I have loved long ago
Joy like a river around me will flow

The Second Coming of Christ

When He shall come with trumpet sound
Oh may I then in Him be found
Clothed in His righteousness alone
Faultless to stand before His Throne
No condemnation now I dread
Jesus and all in Him is mine
Alive in Him my risen head
And clothed in righteousness divine
Bold I approach the eternal throne
And claim the crown, through Christ my own

So I appreciate the wonderful repository of faith, hope, love and assurance to be found in poetry, verse and hymnology. It may be that others will also be helped.

Theological Education

In pages 61 to 65 I tell of the time at Clifton Theological College and the challenge of reading theology.

The G.O.E. course was tested over ten to twelve papers and marked at Oxford or Cambridge to the level of a "Pass" degree. I gladly applied my mind to the work.

Reading letters I sent to Mary during my first year

(Oct 1961 – June 1962) it's fascinating that I say

"I don't want to be sidetracked about studies as a whole; but knowing the requirements for Ministry, i.e. a love for the Lord, for prayer, for His Word and being filled with the Holy Spirit, this must come first, I have three years I want to put to the best advantage." I write...

"Sometimes I find myself a bit lost with it all, the G.O.E. course will be good, but without prayer and the ministry of His Word it will be utterly futile.

I am thankful for godly tutors who believe in the authority of the Bible."

The beauty of the Bible

Looking back over my life I thank God for those early days of confidence in the Bible. I didn't possess my own Bible until I purchased one from Bagsters Bible Bookshop (Page 44). Bible study gatherings at the YMCA, the preaching of Dr Martyn Lloyd-Jones, the ministry of John Stott, Jim Packer at Eclectics, all helped my confidence in preaching from the Bible.

Billy Graham (1918–2018) writes "In 1949 I had been having a great many doubts concerning the Bible" he "wrestled with God " and said "Here and now, by faith, I accept the Bible as thy Word. I take it all". It changed his ministry. he found himself saying "The Bible says" "The Bible says" and people responded to the authority of God's Word

The Ordination Service sets out the condition for success in the Ministry; the need to know the Bible. "that, by daily reading and weighing of the Scriptures you may wax riper and stronger in your ministry."

Apologetics. – A reasoned defence.

I have always been impressed by those who have a grasp of apologetics, who can readily present a rational answer to the most searching questions of the agnostics and atheists. C.S.Lewis, Alister McGrath, Ravi Zacharias, and others. .

Doctrine Outlines are helpful: Four Aspects of History.
1. Age of innocence,
2. The Fall,
3. Salvation History,
4. Restoration,
Origin, Meaning, Morality, Destiny

Or C. S .Lewis' "Into the light of utter actuality.

That Presence Immediate, Palpable and Unavoidable,

Or Isaac Watts 'Where reason fails with all her powers, there Faith prevails and love adores.

George MacDonald's "The heart that is not yet sure of its God is afraid to laugh in His presence.

I enjoy reading the serious stuff even if I don't retain much!

'A faithful guide to Philosophy' by Peter S. Williams. C. S. Lewis versus the New Atheists

In College days I never really got into the minds of Liberal theologians or the Graf-Wellhausen hypothesis of the writing of the Pentateuch .

C.S.Lewis says that theology is like a map – a map based upon the experiences of many people – it won't necessarily get you to God but could help to sort out wrong, bad or muddled out of date ideas of Him.

Mere Christianity Bk iv ch.1

Doctrine /Theology

Was helpful in sorting out Infant Baptism with the teaching of The Covenant.

Atonement. The penal substitutional theory of the Atonement I found helpful.

I read somewhere of a learned professor who when asked what profound doctrine had he discovered through theology replied

"I found the dear Lord Jesus" Amen,

And finally I go back to 1 Cor 13 'Now I know in part, then shall I know as I am known.'

ACKNOWLEDGEMENTS

I would like to thank those who have been involved in helping to get my memoirs into print, especially Chris Powell and Verité CM Ltd; my daughter Marina for her IT skills, and her friend Sarah Lomas who made the comment, 'You ought to write your memoirs, George' as we holidayed on the Isles of Scilly; my wife, Mary, for typing some of my rough notes; Robert Ben-Nathan, my school friend, himself an author, for his encouragement. Also Andrew Chamberlain and Ali Hull for their helpful suggestions at the Lee Abbey writers' course in 2014, and David Leigh for his excellent photographic ability.

Thanks to Trevor Partington, David Barker, Doug Grounds, Myra Leslie, David Griffiths, David Stanbury, William Parker, Geoff Cashmore, Joan Anslow and Pat Doyle who responded to my 'How do you see me?' request!

Adrian Whitfield QC, for his help with some official documents.

And all those, who over the years, have been frustrated at my comments about 'writing my memoirs'. For any who should have been mentioned here but are not – I apologise!